FIND
BANKS

A Honley house, a family business and a lost community

Angela Marshall

HONLEY CIVIC SOCIETY

FINDING BANKS

Published in England by Honley Civic Society

Printed by Enterprise Print, Honley

© Angela Marshall and Honley Civic Society

Text by Angela Marshall

Design PFM

First published 2020

ISBN-13   978-1-9997663-5-1

Banks House 14 Banks Honley

Doing genealogy is not a cold gathering of facts but, instead, a breathing
of life into all who have gone before. We are the storytellers of the tribe. All
tribes have one. We have been called, as if it were, by our genes. Those
who have gone before cry out to us, "Tell our story!" so we do.

From *The Chosen* by Della M. Cummings Wright

Edited and reworded as *The Storyteller* by Tom Dunn, 1943

FINDING BANKS

A Honley house, a family business and a lost community

Contents   **page**

BANKS HOUSE, BANKS, HONLEY, APRIL 2018

The bank and access to
the top garden above

The bank, looking
up to number 16

One of the Edward
Holdroyd & Sons Ltd signs
which we discovered
and had on show
for many years

A PERSONAL INTRODUCTION

In early 2018, whilst having a clearout, I opened a package of papers that had been returned to us from the bank ten years earlier when the mortgage on our house was repaid. Astonishingly, the package contained copies of some old legal documents relating to various property agreements concerning Banks, Honley and specifically to our house, 'Banks House' at number 14. Their appearance prompted further research to learn about the history of the house and the immediate area that, for many years, comprised the joinery business of Edward Holdroyd & Sons. It quickly became a fascinating project; every new piece of information led down another path or provided another piece of the jigsaw. Pulling the threads together became utterly absorbing.

Around this time also, the BBC was showing *A House Through Time*, a documentary in which historians had painstakingly researched everyone who had lived in a house in Liverpool from the time it had been built in the 1840s to the present. The team had delved into the minutiae of the lives of each resident, sometimes perhaps to the point of intrusion. Whilst I was interested in the people who had lived at Banks, I am not an academic and was not planning to make it a major project. Almost all the information I gathered was already in the public domain, it was just a case of gathering the relevant pieces together. It was also a means of showing that actually anyone with a bit of time to spare can do the same.

The availability of information is inevitably limited. It is not possible to learn everything about the past and sometimes a best guess is all that can be managed. However, these guesses are probably not that far from the truth. There will be mistakes, I can only apologise in advance of these becoming apparent, but I had to stop somewhere! A project such as this is never going to be completed. As more information becomes available, it can only ever be a work in progress!

We moved to Banks House, Banks in late 1986. It was our third house in six years and the prospect of a possible lifetime of regular moves was a little depressing. We could never have imagined still being in it over 30 years later. Actually, we were still young and could never have imagined being 30 years older! During our first days in Honley we briefly considered changing the name of the property but decided to keep it because first, it was painted onto the front door, second, it actually sounded quite impressive and third, the mortgage that stretched endlessly ahead of us meant that the property was ... the Bank's that is!

We knew from the outset about the joinery business. We had seen an old photograph of the workforce gathered outside the original offices. We had unearthed a couple of old sign boards when we cleared the garden. We had puzzled over a stone slab table in one of two small keeping cellars. It was the discovery of one of the signs that read, 'Edward Holdroyd & Sons, Joiners, Building Contractors and Funeral Directors' that prompted the swift removal of the table ... just in case!

We took down the original wooden gates across the drive, huge and very heavy, and cut the solid 10 x 10 inch wooden gate posts down to a manageable level. These all contributed to an ever increasing woodpile, along with five big sycamores that did little more than block out light. We removed all evidence of old plumbing in an outhouse and learned to live with the very steep drop into the cellar; the result of historic structural changes made within a limited space. Over the years, we made many changes to the house to meet our own preferences and the needs of a family of three, then four, not giving much thought to who had occupied it before us.

Perhaps, only when we had the bathroom refitted in 2007 and had to break up the old, vast, impractical pot bath, did we speculate on how it might have got there. We used to joke that it must have been hung on a crane whilst the house was built around it. The plumber commented that such baths were only installed during a brief period around 1905, leading us to conclude that the kitchen and bathroom above it must have been added to the house some 25 or so years after the date we had originally believed it to have been built.

All home improvements came with their challenges, uneven stone floors, creaking floorboards, antiquated plumbing and out-of-date electric cables, lath and plaster ceilings, stone walls that are filled with rubble and sometimes covered in a mixture of cement and horse hair, at least 18 inches in depth – sometimes more and never truly straight. There is also evidence of long past subsidence, but the house is built on solid rock so is going nowhere.

We had wanted a house with 'character' but what of one with history?

In the early days, we even considered contacting an elderly Mr Holdroyd, who allegedly still lived somewhere on Far Banks, to ask some questions; but of course we didn't and then we decided it would be too late to do so. So, the discovery of the paperwork rekindled old questions about the age of the house, its owners and its occupants.

Deciphering key facts from the elegant but sometimes minutely handwritten legal documents and the complex terminology used in them was challenging, but provided some really useful information. Names and details were then cross referenced where possible with information found on the absolutely invaluable *Ancestry* website [1], without which this project would not have been possible. Maps were also found on the *Huddersfield Exposed Mapping Project* website[2] covering the years 1854 to 1950.

Also of significant interest were a number of the books produced by Honley Civic Society, which provided context to some of the developments and events that would have been taking place in our village during the period under review. Lastly, some additional information came from discussions with David and Janet Stringer who came to Banks a few years before we did. Then a chance encounter with Julian Holdroyd enabled a few more gaps to be filled in. All of these have been extremely valuable.

However, no record of earlier life in Honley can be complete without an acknowledgement to the work of Mary Jagger. Mrs Jagger was born in December 1849, the daughter of Honley postmaster John Tilburn and his wife Mary. She married Samuel Jagger, a factory manager and woollen salesman from Armitage Bridge in November 1879 at St Mary's Church, Honley. Much of her life was spent on Far End Lane, then Southgate, just along the road from Banks. Her book, *The History of Honley and its Hamlets from the Earliest Time to the Present* was published in 1914.[3]

In her preface, Mrs Jagger notes

No greater calamity can happen to nations or persons than to lose all knowledge of their past. Indigenous to Honley soil, love for my native place has prompted me to write its history before old scenes fade into the background and the old is changed to the new.

She goes on to say

A country would have no history to record if it was not for the type of men and women brought under review in this publication, who held to the place of their birth, dwelling side by side, and bound together by ties of common birth and speech.

Honley, some four miles south of Huddersfield and three miles north of Holmfirth, is mentioned in the Domesday Book

In Haneleia (Honley) and Meltham, Cola and Suuen held four carucates of land to be taxed where three ploughs might be employed. Ilbert now has it, but it is waste.

So Mrs Jagger records our first glimpse of Honley as a place which had been given a name to distinguish it from other places.

Hane (Hone) means dwelling, leia (ley) an open space in a wood, thus the word indicates a dwelling or clearing in a wood.

Mrs Jagger takes us through Honley's ancient history, via the Middle Ages, on to the Industrial Revolution, passing the Luddite uprising which touched Honley briefly but significantly enough to become absorbed into its story. This record picks up some of the threads and looks more closely at the last 200 years in the life of one small part of Honley village - Banks. Home to a few, but unfamiliar to many. For some, little more than a short cut between the main road and the village, to miss out the traffic lights at Honley Bridge!

The old scenes have already faded into the background and the old is most definitely changed to the new but, if you look hard enough, the long shadows of the past are still there. You can see a place daily, but never really know about it until you actually stop and let the past overtake you for a while, so that it comes, briefly, into view.

Angela Marshall
September 2020

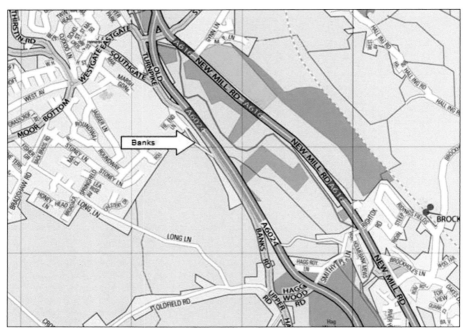

Map of part of Honley[4]

The cottages at Banks in 1976, the sign BANKS on number
2 is the only indication of a place name

FINDING BANKS

B anks is part of a single road that changes its name several times within a fairly short distance. To add to the confusion, these names are often applied in different places subject to the mapping service used. Name changes have also been introduced at different times. In the very early 1800s, the road formed part of the main turnpike route from Honley to Holmfirth.

From the centre of Honley village, the very narrow road that heads south, squeezing past the building at the corner of Marsh, used to be Far End Lane. It became Southgate in 1897, connecting as it does with Westgate, Eastgate and Church Street. For the benefit of any visitors to Honley, Northgate is about half a mile away, up Station Road and just past the railway station and the High School. It climbs the hill until it meets the road between Farnley Tyas and Castle Hill, Almondbury.

Southgate stretches a short distance, passing the theatre which is housed in the building that used to be the Sunday school and a car park which was formerly the site of the 1842 Primitive Chapel to which it was attached. Where Southgate meets the Old Turnpike road up from Honley Bridge, just by the road up to Honley Cricket Ground and what was Far End House, it picks up its original name of Far End Lane. After another few metres, Far End Lane diverts off into Field End Lane and the road to a farm. Field End Lane also leads to a narrow track that we refer to as 'the back lane'. In fact, the old maps actually call it Back Lane. This runs for a short distance along the back of Banks, providing access to the fields for the farmer and to the rear of number 16, before becoming a footpath that eventually leads back down, via a set of steps, onto the road just beyond 48 Far Banks.

From Far End Lane, the road continues as Banks, sometimes referred to as Banks, Far End Lane. It passes the houses at *Ryecroft*, *Netherfield* and then three newer detached properties set back from the road, before reaching its only official form of identification, a sign that reads BANKS on the wall of the first of a terrace of cottages, number 2. After the old properties, 2 to 14, and another three detached bungalows, 16 to 20, also set back and higher up, the road becomes Far Banks, starting with a house built in 2003 and numbered, somewhat incongruously, 36. A row of five terraced houses, 40 to 48 are identified as FAR BANKS. These are then followed by several more individual properties that take us half a mile to the junction with the road to Oldfield at Upper Hagg. As Far Banks gets higher, so too do the houses, numbers 80 and 82 having more steps up to their front doors than can be practical. A helpful sign on a gate advises anyone making a delivery to drive round onto the Oldfield road to locate them from the rear.

The question of the property numbering had perplexed us since our arrival in Honley. With a gap between numbers 20 and 40, it was clear that there must at one time have been something between Banks and Far Banks but, whatever it was, there was nothing left of it. The eventual

Hope Bank Pleasure Grounds viewed from Far Banks across to Brockholes

discovery of a lost community was extremely satisfying. It inevitably widened the scope of the original project allowing past history to be rediscovered.

It wasn't just the numbering. Confusion around the road names has plagued us since we moved here. Despite attempts to change it, the local street map shows us as being on Far End Lane with Banks Road running along the back. Even the map on page 8 shows yet another location for the nonexistent Banks Road, placing it where Far Banks is. Unsurprisingly this confusion, and the proximity to us of 14 Far End Lane, has challenged numerous visitors. To avoid some of the difficulties, we eventually had a sign made for our house that reads, *Banks House, 14 Bank*s. We like to think that this helps.

The A6024 Woodhead Road runs parallel to Banks, sitting a few feet below and separated by a wooded slope. Just beyond it winds the river that gives the Holme Valley its name. The Huddersfield & Woodhead Turnpike was a 14-mile toll road passing through Lockwood, Honley, Holmfirth, Holmbridge, Holme and over Holme Moss to reach Woodhead in north Derbyshire. It reportedly opened in 1768 when, from Lockwood, the route originally climbed Taylor Hill Road to reach Berry Brow. However, this was replaced in around 1809 with a lower-level valley road between Lockwood and Honley.[5] The newer road through Thongsbridge to Holmfirth was built a few years later.

In July 2014, Woodhead Road was included on the route when the Grand Départ of the Tour de France international cycle race came to Yorkshire. The people of Honley, like everyone else in the county embraced the event with typical enthusiasm. On 6th July, the road was completely closed to non-tour traffic, allowing freedom of movement not known in recent years. Naturally, we took the opportunity to get our bikes out and cycle to Holmfirth to make the most of this rarity. Along its entire distance from Huddersfield to Woodhead, the road was lined with thousands of spectators. There were an estimated 60,000 people on Holme Moss alone. This exciting, joyous, inspirational and colourful spectacle was, almost certainly, the finest moment in its history.

However, the area is not entirely unused to the limelight that comes from attracting visitors. Between 1895 and 1955, the land across the road from Far Banks, between Woodhead Road and the A616 New Mill Road through Brockholes, was the site of the Hope Bank Pleasure Ground. This was the project of John William Mellor, a Honley man, who transformed the Banks Estate, which had been left empty after the closure of the Banks Mills, into a major tourist attraction. People travelled from far and wide to enjoy its formal gardens or to delight in innovative rides and attractions. They spent time on the boating lake, either rowing themselves around in one of a number of former ship's lifeboats, or travelling in the capable hands of the skipper of the steamer *Nil Desperandum*.

In its heyday, Hope Bank brought visitors to Honley in their thousands. Ray Masson's book *Hope Bank Honley's Pleasure Grounds and Gardens*, published by Honley Civic Society, provides a detailed account of this significant, but surprisingly unknown part of Honley's history.[6] In recent years this, together with projects spearheaded by the Holmfirth Sharing Memories group, has encouraged older and newer generations to work together to ensure that the stories about it don't disappear forever.

John William Mellor died in 1927, but his family continued to run his Pleasure Grounds until 1943 when they sold the site to Fred Thompson of Blackpool for £8,790. During the Second World War it was used as a military base and Mr Thompson had to then spend around £20,000 to bring it back into use. Success was limited and the 28½ acre site was eventually sold to Brook Motors, who built a factory there that opened in 1958. They too have since moved on. The industrial estate that now sits in the valley bottom is mostly hidden by trees. Some of these are the poplars that John Mellor had had planted to screen his attraction from outside view. It has long been a source of profound regret that we arrived in Honley about 60 years too late to witness the original spectacle.

The Tour de France passes Banks in 2014

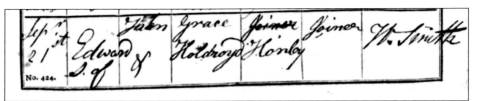

The birth record showing that John Holdroyd was a joiner in 1817

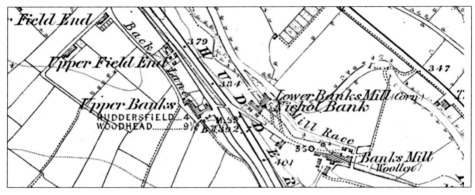

The 1854 Ordnance Survey map shows what is now Banks in relation to Banks mills

The circle shows the original cottages from 2 to 8

BANKS: 1817 TO 1870

Completing some family history research a few years ago led to huge admiration for whoever made the decision back in the early 19th century to start keeping census records. These records started at the beginning of the 1800s as a means of identifying the numbers of available men in the event of their being needed to fight for their country in the Napoleonic Wars of 1803 to 1815. They also served as an approximate headcount to inform plans to ration food stocks in the event of an invasion. It took some years for census records to be collated that might be of greatest use to future seekers of information about people and places. Consequently the *Ancestry* website only provides the census records from 1841. From that year they were then taken at ten year intervals and are the source of vast amounts of information about people, their families, ages, occupations and where they lived. At the time of writing, only records up to and including the 1911 census are accessible[1], as are electoral registers and many birth, marriage, death, probate and travel records. Respect for the living means that census records are not publicly available for 100 years, so – for the purpose of this research – 1911 is as far as they go.

For this record, a logical place to start is 200 years ago, specifically September 1817. Three months earlier, George Taylor of Honley had led a crowd of workers from the Holme Valley towards Huddersfield, declaring that all England had risen to secure their liberties. 'The rich would be poor and the poor would be rich'. History records that they were met by Captain John Armytage and his recently formed Huddersfield Yeomanry.[7] The rebellion was quashed and life continued as before for most people, although the year did see a continuation of Luddite attacks in and around Honley that have remained a significant part of its history.

Meanwhile, at Upper Banks, 21st September, 1817 saw the birth of Edward Holdroyd to parents John and Grace. The record shows that John Holdroyd was already a joiner. Later information gives the official date of the establishment of the Holdroyd business as 1817, although it may be older, especially if John's own father had also been a joiner. Mary Jagger's 1914 publication notes the Holdroyds as being 'over 100 years in the trade'.

It has to be noted that in early records the names Holdroyd and Holroyd are often confused. Indeed on the October 1809 marriage record for John and Grace (nee Lockwood), the registrar has written 'Holroyd', but John has signed his name below as 'Holdroyd'. The error appears again on the 1841 census, by which time Edward 'Holroyd' was aged 24 and living with his widowed mother Grace, still at Upper Banks, Honley. It's likely that other children had already left home as the record shows only two other family members, Benjamin aged 20 and John aged 3, although relationships are not given. The census also gives Edward's occupation as a joiner, indicating that he had taken over his late father's business.

Edward Holdroyd 1817 -1870

A hand drawn map of Honley in 1838 (*page 16*), reproduced in the *Honley Town Book – 1746 to 1846*[8], identifies two distinct developments of buildings, marking the land elevation in between them as Meal Hill. It also shows the surrounding areas of land, many with names that have survived to modern times. The 1854 Ordnance Survey map on page 12 also shows the two developed areas, identifying the larger one as Upper Banks. This name, however, was used in records for both developments, doubtless to distinguish them from the cottages at Lower Banks in the valley below. The larger part of Upper Banks comprised a collection of 12 stone-built terraced houses, later to be identified as the missing numbers 16 to 38. They originally occupied the area between Banks and Far Banks, that is, where 20 Banks and 36 Far Banks now stand.

From information in later census records, it is apparent that the Holdroyds were actually living in the smaller of the two sites, at what is now Banks and at the house that would later be identified as number 4. The separate building to the immediate south-east of the row of cottages is probably the Holdroyd workshop.

Edward married Sarah Ann Moss in November 1842 and, in 1851, the Holdroyd family were all at Upper Banks where joiner Edward employed three men and two apprentices. There were six children recorded on the census, John William, aged 13, being the eldest and evidently one of the apprentices. His appearance on the previous census had suggested a much younger brother, but he was in fact Edward and Sarah Ann's son, born five years before they married. The record of John William's birth in 1837 shows a location of Smithy

Place. This is a few hundred yards towards Holmfirth and connects the Woodhead Road with Brockholes. It was also the address of Sarah Ann's family.

That Sarah Ann was not with Edward on the 1841 census may be explained by the fact that their second child was also born prior to the marriage and that at the time of the census she was at Ridings, near to Smithy Place in Brockholes. With her was a one-year-old son, Edwin Moss, who may actually have been a newborn child. By 1851, Edwin Holdroyd, aged 10, is clearly shown as the second child of Edward and Sarah Ann. Whatever the order that these key events may have occurred in, by 1851 Edward Holdroyd & Sons now officially existed.

The Holdroyds were not the most prominent family living at Upper Banks. The 1841 census identified 15 separate households there, of which six were occupied by constituent parts of the Bray family. Ann Bray and her two children appear to have been next door to the Holdroyds being in the end cottage that would become number 2, whilst the specific whereabouts of the families of John, Thomas, Lucy, David and James are less clear.

Of most significance to the future of Banks was John Bray, a 50-year-old wool carder, living with his wife Grace and their eight children. These included Lavinia aged 25, and 18-year-old Hamer. John died in 1853 but, looking ahead, Lavinia would be at number 8 and Hamer at number 16 for many years, so these may have been the properties that family members had occupied. Other residents at Upper Banks at this time were Simeon and Mary Smith and their seven children, Edward and Lydia Jillott and their nine, as well as Benjamin Holdroyd and his family and the Schofields.

The third family who are of significance to the early Banks story are the Middletons. In 1841 farmer John Middleton and his wife Hannah and son Walter were living half a mile away from Banks at Upper Hagg. The *Honley Town Book*, which reproduces the Parish records from 1746 to 1846, shows that in 1839 John Middleton of Upper Hagg was appointed as one of two Overseers of the Poor. This position, created by the Poor Laws, carried the responsibility for ministering to the needs of the poor by collecting taxes from the parish and distributing money or food to those most in need.

John's son, Walter, who had been born in 1823, moved from Upper Hagg to Wolfstones following his marriage to 29-year-old Ann Boothroyd from Netherthong in June 1850. By 1861, they were back living at Upper Hagg with their four children, Ellen, Mary, Emma and John. Walter had presumably taken over the house and work from his father as the 1861 census records his occupation as a farmer of 27 acres. Walter's parents, John and Hannah Middleton, were aged 59 and 60. From the information available it appears that, having retired, they were living at a newly-built house on Upper Banks that would later be numbered as 14 Banks and, later still, be named as 'Banks House'. We cannot know for certain when the house was built. It is not apparent on the 1854 map, although mapping for this actually took place in 1847, but we can assume that, as the Middletons were in it in 1861, that it was built during the mid 1850s. This made the house about 30 years older than we had actually supposed it to be.

Three households along from John and Hannah Middleton, Edward and Sarah Ann Holdroyd now had ten children living at home. John William had married Edna Wood in May 1860 and was living on Westgate, possibly near to her father's grocery shop. It is likely to have been during the preceding years that the Banks property was enlarged. This was achieved by

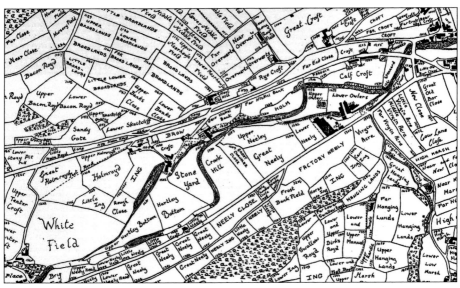

A map frpm the Wormald survey of Honley in 1838, also
showing the lands owned by Ann Walker.

The rental valuation for the Walker lands from 1826,

joining it with its neighbour and removing internal walls to create more spacious rooms. The transformation of two properties into one is indicated by a window where a door evidently once existed.

Edwin, now aged 21, had joined his father and brother to be a joiner and cabinet maker, whilst sisters, Mary and Martha were dressmakers. Other children of the family were Joseph, Benjamin, Allen, Emily, George and Fred and eight-year-old Charley. They all have their own story, having their own lives, work and descendants; but only a few of them fall within the primary focus of this book. However, many of these names can be found on gravestones in Honley's cemetery.

It was inevitable at that time that any sons of Edward Holdroyd or of John Middleton should follow them into their respective family businesses, but for the daughters and for most of the other inhabitants of Upper Banks, employment was often found either in domestic service or in one of the local mills.

There were two mills at Lower Banks; the Corn Mill and the Woollen Mill. In *Wool and Worsit – a History of Textiles in the Holme Valley*[9], Michael Day records that the earliest information about these comes from an Indenture, or contract, dated 1st January, 1768, between William Walker of Halifax and Joseph Armitage and Joseph Jagger of Honley. Each man contributed towards the cost of building 'mills for the crushing and pressing of rapes with sufficient granaries storehouses and other buildings and improving the fulling mill there now standing'. Fulling was a step in the process of woollen cloth making which involved cleaning it to eliminate oils, dirt and other impurities. The indenture also includes permission to build 'a rasp or other engine on the premises for cutting, clipping, rasping or grinding dyeing wood'. Power for the new rape mill was to be taken from the water wheel in the fulling mill.

Josephs Armitage and Jagger were to rent the premises from William Walker by paying him a sum equal to the interest on the money he would have earned had it been invested, plus a fee of 5% for a term of 42 years. Honley Civic Society has confirmed that William Walker was the grandfather of Ann Walker, later of Crownest Park, Halifax. After his death William's properties, including the Banks Mills, passed to his son John and later to Ann following the death of her brother John, the last male heir, in 1830. In 1838, a survey of Honley undertaken and published by Samuel Wormald showed the fields and land along with their ownership for rental purposes. It confirms that some of the Banks properties, including Ryecroft, were owned by Ann Walker.

Ann later moved from Crownest to live with her partner Anne Lister at Shibden Hall, Halifax. The story of non-conformist Anne Lister (referred to by many as 'Gentleman Jack') is well recorded and has been the subject of television dramas, information having been taken from her often coded but particularly detailed diaries. In one of these, dated August 1837, Ms Lister records making a visit to Mr John Haigh and identifying him as a 'tenant to Ann for her Honley Mills'.

By 1845 the mills were being run by the Haigh family with John Haigh responsible for paying the rents. Financial records for 1844 note that the income from Banks Mill on the River Holme and other properties amounted to £320. However, by this time ill health meant that Ann was no longer able to manage her affairs which were being conducted by her brother-in-law, George Mackay Sutherland, from Shibden Hall where Ann had been living

Old Corn Mil at Banks

Old Cottage at Banks

with Anne Lister until the latter's death. Despite this, in the Great Holmfirth Flood of 1852, when the woollen mill was damaged, records of The Holme Reservoir Commissioners show Ann Walker to still be the identified owner. When she died in 1854 her estates, including Banks, were left to Ewan Charles Sutherland, her sister Elizabeth's son.

At the time of the 1844 financial records the owner of the Lower Mill or corn mill had been William Robinson, with chief rent payments being made to him in respect of land on the 'Bank's Estate, Honley'. It must have closed down shortly after this as by the time Mary Jagger began writing about the corn mill, it was already a ruin. Her reference paints a somewhat improbably idyllic picture of the mill 'nestling in the once sylvan hollow beside the stream'.[3] However, the 'slumberous peacefulness of the hollow' was still being disturbed by the Banks Woollen Mill a short distance away. As noted, by the 1850s, this was being run by members of the Haigh family from Hall Ing, trading as John Haigh & Co. In March 1860, their partnership was dissolved and the mill was then run by William Haigh, who lived at Far End House on Far End Lane. He also built a residence near to the mills, naming it 'Hope Bank'. The woollen mill and others in the vicinity appear to have provided a variety of jobs and created much of the employment for the people of Upper Banks and the surrounding area.

William Haigh appears to have had a number of difficulties during his time as manager of Banks Mill, instigating several claims against people that were not then upheld. There are a couple of references to the 'Holroyds' in the Banks Mill record within Alan Brooke's *Catalogue of the Textile Mills and Factories of the Huddersfield area c.1790-1914*[10]. In 1864, William Haigh took the business to the County Court where he 'prosecutes Holroyd for non return of 10 skeps, value £4'. However, 'Holroyd shows receipt' and Haigh 'looses the case'. The same article notes 'Edward Holroyd and Sons, joiners, builders, cabinet makers' to be in the mill's 1881 Directory.

Finally, at 2.00am on Saturday 30th May, 1868 Banks Mill was destroyed by fire. No explanation of how the fire occurred was given, but the building was then left untenanted for several years. The path from it through to Smithy Place was closed due to the danger from the building and, according to the poetic Mrs Jagger, 'time and nature softened the gaunt looks of the wrecked mill'. An advertisement appeared in the *Huddersfield Chronicle* in April 1869 for -

the house, farm buildings, meal mill, 8 cottages, the remaining portions of the woollen mill, and around 55 acres of land commonly known as Banks mill to be let[9].

Interest was evidently minimal as it would be a number of years before any actual change took place. The mill's own records conclude with 7th May, 1887, 'Banks Mill and Lower Banks Mill and estate to be sold'. The final record that follows is for 6th July, 1889, whch states, 'Mill and ground to be sold plus estate at Hope Bank, house and farm'.[10] Six years later the area would be the site of John William Mellor's Hope Bank Pleasure Ground.

There is something of a conflict in the views of this particular development. Mary Jagger notes that-

Mr J. W. Mellor eventually purchased the property, and has gradually changed the picturesque hollow to a modern pleasure resort named after his residence.

However, in his book on the history of Hope Bank, Ray Masson notes that Mr Mellor is said to have described his new tract of land as 'a wild, howling wilderness'! [6]

In Memory of
SARAH ANN
THE BELOVED WIFE OF
EDWARD HOLDROYD
OF BANKS, HONLEY
WHO DIED MARCH 11TH 1862
AGED 44 YEARS

ALSO WILLIE, THEIR SON
WHO DIED FEB 21ST 1863
AGED 11 MONTHS

ALSO THE ABOVE NAMED
EDWARD HOLDROYD
WHO DIED MAY 16TH 1870
AGED 53 YEARS

HE SUFFERED MUCH BUT MURMER'D NOT
WE WATCHED HIM DAY BY DAY
GROW LESS AND LESS WITH ACHING HEARTS
UNTIL HE PASSED AWAY

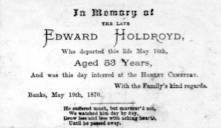

In Memory of
THE LATE
EDWARD HOLDROYD,
Who departed this life May 16th,
Aged 53 Years,
And was this day interred at the HONLEY CEMETERY.
With the Family's kind regards.
Banks, May 19th, 1870.

He suffered much, but murmur'd not,
We watched him day by day,
Grow less and less with aching hearts,
Until he passed away.

HOLDROYD Edward. 7 July Effects under £450

The Will of Edward Holdroyd late of Honley in the
Parish of Almondbury in the County of York Joiner
deceased who died 16 May 1870 at Honley aforesaid
was proved at Wakefield by the oaths of John William
Moss of Neileys in Honley aforesaid Joiner and George
Brooke of Honley aforesaid Joiner the Executors. [1]

This original Holdroyd cart was used during the first half of the 20th century by Edward Holdroyd and Sons of Honley and is on display in the Tolson Memorial Museum, Ravensknowle Park, Huddersfield

BANKS: 1870 TO 1890

E dward Holdroyd died on 16th May, 1870 aged 53. Like many of the Holdroyds, his grave can be found in Honley Cemetery. The text on the gravestone shows that his wife, Sarah Ann, had died eight years earlier, probably in childbirth. The baby, a son named Willie, is shown to have died 11 months after her. They were clearly hard times. Despite Edward's death, for another century his name would live on in the joinery business he had created.

In the 1871 census John William Holdroyd, now aged 33, is described as a master joiner, employing four men and four boys as joiners. He, his wife Edna and their family were living at Upper Banks. A joiner's shop is recorded in between properties occupied by Michael Bray and John Middleton. The family of John Middleton's son, Walter, had also moved to Upper Banks, although Walter is not actually shown on the census. In his absence, Ann was recorded as the head of the family. Ellen had left to marry William Beaumont; Mary was a woollen weaver, Emma was a 17-year-old dressmaker, John was 13 and another child, Walter (junior), was nine-years-old.

The addresses given are confusingly variable. Banks, Upper Banks, Far Banks and Back Lane are all used at different times to refer to properties between Far End Lane or Field End and Upper Banks. At this time, the name Banks also referred to the area in the valley below, where the mills were. So, when the 1871 census recorded that John William Holdroyd was living at Upper Banks and Edwin Holdroyd was at Banks, further clarification is needed.

The census generally records properties in the order that they appear. John William Holdroyd and his family appeared on the census return that covered District 7. This recorded each house from Marsh in the centre of Honley, via Far End Lane on its south-west side (the even numbers), past the Primitive Methodist Chapel and Far End House to Upper Banks. The conclusion reached, from matching properties to known information, is that, at this time, John William and Edna Holdroyd, identified as living at Upper Banks, had actually taken over the cottage that would become 4 Banks following his father's death the previous year.

Edwin Holdroyd and his wife Sarah-Ann (nee France), whom he had married in July 1861, appeared on the District 4 return. This recorded properties from Smithy Place to Banks, where the mills were before crossing the Woodhead Road and picking up Far End Lane on its north-east side (the odd numbers) past the post office where Mary Tilburn lived and The Wheatsheaf Inn and on into the village centre. Edwin and Sarah Ann were living with their three children at Banks, in a cottage that was close to the old mills. Their neighbour was a shoe-maker, Henry Schofield and his family. The census recorded the next property along from them to be Banks Woollen Mill noting that it had 'burnt down' and beyond that was Banks Mill (Corn Mill) and another neighbour, William Hirst, a corn miller.

The houses at Upper Banks would later be numbered from 16 to 38 'Far Banks', whilst those at numbers 2 to 14 became just 'Banks'. The older of these latter properties might have originally been connected to the Banks Mills, sitting below them in the valley. If they had been tied cottages, this might explain the single word 'BANKS' on number 2. They may even be some of the cottages referred to in the 1869 advertisement for the sale of Banks Mill. When they were built, the row would have comprised five small cottages. They are now the oldest part of Banks, already in evidence on the 1838 map and probably built around the time of the construction of the original Turnpike road.

In 1871, John William Holdroyd's neighbours were Mary Smith, James Stott, John Greaves and Michael and Hannah Bray. A few yards nearer to Upper Banks and just beyond the joiners' shop in between them, were John and Hannah Middleton.

At this time, George Brook, Edward Holdroyd's son-in-law and one of his executors, was living a short distance away on Far End Lane with his wife Mary and their daughter. With them were siblings Charley and Emily Holdroyd, listed as George's brother-in-law and sister-in-law. Charley and Emily must have had to move out of their family home when their brother John brought his family to live there following their father's death. We can only speculate on whether this was all agreed amicably or not, but it may have been especially difficult for Charley who would soon find a way to move back to his childhood home. However, it should be noted that the apparent movement of family members between households seemed to be a fairly common occurrence.

Another ten years on and the 1881 census shows that John William Holdroyd and his family were still at Banks, but now at Quarry House, which is just below Banks on the Woodhead Road, a short distance south of the Jacob's Well pub and Honley Bridge. In 1881 it would indeed have overlooked a sandstone quarry. It is an impressive property that may well have been built by Holdroyds and would have been appropriate for the eldest of Edward Holdroyd's sons.

The house was also connected directly to Banks by a short but steep footpath up the wooded slope between the two roads. With the options of walking to Banks either via the Old Turnpike, or by way of the slip road at Upper Banks, the creation of this stepped and, if it were not for the handrail, slightly precarious footpath would have saved a significant amount of time and effort between home and work. A bus stop is now sited at the foot of the path as this short cut up to Banks is still in regular use.

Edwin Holdroyd was still living at Banks with Sarah-Ann and seven of their children. Banks in this instance still referred to the cottages at Lower Banks near to the old mills. Edwin, by then aged 48, was a joiner and contractor, employing four men and three boys. It should be noted that in several census records each of the Holdroyd brothers identified himself as the employer of the Holdroyd's workforce. However, it is more likely that as partners in the business each had his own specific team of men.

A short distance away, at Upper Banks, John and Edwin's younger brother Charley was living with his wife, Emma Letitia (nee Schofield) and their three children, six-year-old Harry, five-year-old Lewis and a two-year-old daughter Ellen. It is apparent that he had moved back into the house vacated by John and Edna, the one where he had grown up and in which he had lived until his father's death a decade earlier.

A few yards from Charley and his family, Walter and Ann Middleton had taken over the house that his parents, John and Hannah Middleton, had been in until John's death in August 1879. They were also sharing their home with their 13-year-old granddaughter,

Florence Beaumont, their daughter Ellen having died three years earlier. The household also included a general servant in 14-year-old Emma Lindley. Their daughter, Emma, had married Arthur Hoyle in December 1876. Eldest son, John, had married Amelia (Milly) Battye in July 1879 and youngest son, Walter, was working as a drayman and was boarding with his employer in Holmfirth. In addition to owning the property they lived in, the Middletons also owned the land around them. On one side this was undeveloped land as well as that on which stood most of the houses at Upper Banks On the other, it comprised the area from where the Holdroyds were running their joinery business.

Apart from the joinery, the Middleton's 1881 neighbours were siblings Hamer Bray, living at what would become 16 Far Banks and Lavinia Bray, at what would become 8 Banks. Lavinia also had her daughter and son-in law, Edna and Allen Jillott, living with her. George Brook was still at Far End Lane, but was by then a widower. Charley having moved on from there to his own home, George was sharing his address with another of his brothers-in-law, Fred Holdroyd. Indeed, Fred appears on several consecutive census records living with different family members each time.

Walter Middleton (senior) died on 9th December, 1886. By this time, especially if health was failing, he and Ann may already have been living with one of their sons, possibly Walter (junior) who had settled at Lane End, Holmfirth, as this is the address on the Probate record. By the time of his death, the house they had lived in at Banks was already being rented out to Edwin and Sarah-Ann Holdroyd and their family, who had moved the short distance across the Woodhead Road from Lower Banks.

In a will dated 3rd December, 1885, Walter had appointed his sons John and Walter (junior) as trustees and executors 'upon trust to permit his wife, Ann Middleton, to have the use of his furniture and household effects and to receive the rents income and profits of his real estate during her life'. Thereafter the rents were to go to his daughter, Emma Hoyle. The will was proved in the Wakefield District Registry of Probate on 28th February, 1887.

It may be assumed that Walter Middleton had retained the 27 acres of land that his father had owned as, at his death, his estate was valued at £1,287 10s 9d. An online check suggests that this could be worth as much as £1,930,000 by today's values.[11] The Middletons were evidently wealthy people.

The steep footpath linking Banks with Woodhead Road, close to Quarry House

The will of Walter Middleton, dated 3rd December, 1885

MIDDLETON Walter.

Personal Estate £1,287 10s. 9d.

28 February.   The Will with a Codicil of Walter Middleton late of Lane End Holmfirth in the County of **York** Railway Carrier who died 9 December 1886 at Lane End was proved at **Wakefield** by John Middleton of Lane End Railway Carrier and Walter Middleton of Moor Lane Netherthong near Huddersfield in the said County Railway Carrier the Sons the Executors.

BANKS: 1890 TO 1900

By the end of the 1880s, Edwin and Charley Holdroyd were both living at Banks with John William a short distance away at Quarry House. George Holdroyd, Edward's youngest son, was living with his in-laws in the valley at Lower Banks. Like his brothers, he was also a joiner. The stage appears to have been set for the expansion of the business of Edward Holdroyd & Sons.

A document drawn up almost a century later outlines a number of historic schedules, one of which is a transfer of land that took place on 4th April, 1888. This was an agreement between (1) Joe Jessop and (2) John William Holdroyd, Edwin Holdroyd, Charley Holdroyd and George Brook. Joe Jessop was a draper with a shop in Church Street and was living at Highfield Terrace in 1881. He had moved to the then newly built Ryecroft, Banks by 1891. Ryecroft was at that time a single house at the junction of Far End Lane, Banks and Field End Lane. By 1904 it had been expanded into three properties, 1, 3 and 5 Ryecroft. A few yards to the south east of Ryecroft, Netherfield was built sometime around 1929 and does not therefore appear until the 1933 map.

Probably around the time that Ryecroft was built and of his move there, Joe Jessop was evidently persuaded to sell some of the land to the Holdroyds. The land being transferred had an area of 1,351 square yards. Its acquisition was part of the expansion of the joinery business into the timber yard of later years. At a later date an additional 1,330 square yards of Ryecroft land would also be bought from the Thornton family.

The census of 1891 shows Edwin, Sarah Ann and ten of their children, aged between 25 and four years and Charley, Emma and their four children all still living at Banks. Charley's sons had now also joined the business as both Harry and Lewis were joiner's apprentices. Like most of those below working age, Ellen was a scholar, as was Charley's youngest child, Norman, who was nine-years-old.

However, in 1885 Charley and Emma had had a second daughter, Beatrice. She died in 1886 at the age of only 18 months and so does not appear on any census records. Her name is the first one on the headstone above a grave in Honley cemetery that would eventually carry the names of other family members. In 1891 Lavinia Bray was still living at number 8 and sharing her home with her daughter and son-in-law, Edna and Allan Jillott. Allan's brother, Wright Jillott, lived next door at number 6 with his wife Sarah and their family. Hamer Bray was still enjoying his lengthy occupation of number 16.

We can't know the reasons for it, but a record in the *London Gazette* [12], dated 26th July, 1892, reported the dissolution of John William Holdroyd's partnership with E Holdroyd and Sons. 'All debts due to and owing by the said Partnership will be received and paid by the said Edwin Holdroyd and Charley Holdroyd'. It is possible that the expansion of the business caused conflict between the brothers. Charley was evidently ambitious which may have presented a challenge to the status of a brother 16 years his senior.

Beatrice Holdroyd 1885 -1886

Developments at Banks

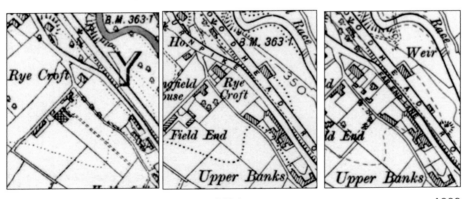

1894   1904   1933

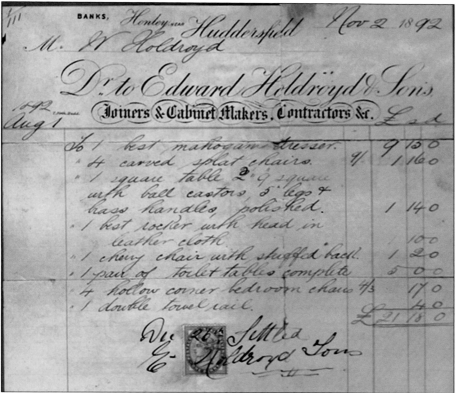

Billhead for Edward Holdroyd and Sons in 1892.
The official notification of the dissolution of the Holdroyd partnership in 1892

THE LONDON GAZETTE, JULY 26, 1892.

NOTICE is hereby given, that the Partnership heretofore subsisting between us the undersigned, John William Holdroyd, Edwin Holdroyd, and Charley Holdroyd, carrying on business as Joiners, Builders, and Contractors, at Banks, Honley, near Huddersfield, in the county of York, under the style or firm of E. Holdroyd and Sons, is hereby dissolved, by mutual consent, so far as regards the said John William Holdroyd, as from the 13th day of July, 1892. All debts due to and owing by the said Partnership will be received and paid by the said Edwin Holdroyd and Charley Holdroyd, by whom the said business will in future be carried on under the style or firm of E. Holdroyd and Sons.—Dated this 13th day of July, 1892.

JOHN WILLIAM HOLDROYD.
EDWIN HOLDROYD.
CHARLEY HOLDROYD.

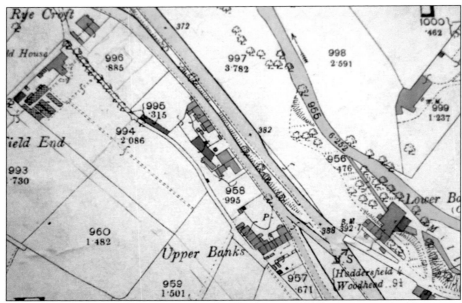

The 1892, Ordnance Survey map showing the house at 14 Banks connected to new premises for Edward Holdroyd & Sons

A page from a ledger of April 1894 and a copy of the list of employees.

Geo H Holdroyd
Holdroyd JWm
Quarmby Charles
Sugden JE
Booth John
Smith Joe
  do, David
Senior Tom
  do, Joe
Kilner Joe
Roodhouse Fred
Heyes JE
Holdroyd Harry
  do, Lewis
  do, Frank
Fred Lindley
Wimpenny Joe
Bower Sam
Booth Willie
  do, Joe
Taylor Walter
Garner Jno

Despite the difficulties, work continued and a receipt dated 2nd November shows that a Mr W Holdroyd (presumably a relative) paid £21 18s for several items of furniture, the most costly being a mahogany dresser. The items appear to have been ordered on 1st August and were paid for by 26th December. Even the receipt looks elegant!

On 2nd March. 1893, eight months after the partnership split, Edwin Holdroyd died. Born in 1841, he was 52 years of age. His sons, Charles Edward and John were identified as his executors.

By 1892, the Ordnance Survey map [13] shows the house at 14 Banks to be connected to new premises for Edward Holdroyd & Sons, along with a number of other buildings at the back that were also part of the joinery business. To the south of it, the 12 properties at Upper Banks can be more clearly seen. The 'P' marked on the map probably indicates the pump or well that would have provided water for the community.

By the end of 1894, the Honley Urban District Council had been formed. This was subdivided into four wards, Central, East, South and West. Banks and its surrounding area fell within the South district. Among those who were elected to serve on the Council were Charley Holdroyd, joiner and builder of Banks, and John Edward Heap.[3] John Heap was a solicitor whose parents ran the local public house, The Wheatsheaf at Far End Lane (later Southgate). In April 1883, he had married Lydia Ann Haigh, the daughter of the late Thomas Haigh, accountant, of Grove House, Gynn Lane.

As a consequence of both the dissolution of the partnership with John and of the death of Edwin, Charley was the Holdroyd now responsible for the joinery business. He appears to have spent the next few years expanding it, both in size and in the services it provided to the people of Honley and beyond.

Letter headings and advertising flyers now read *Edward Holdroyd & Sons (Charley Holdroyd)* as he sought to increase his overall stake in the firm. In acknowledgment of new beginnings, an impressive wages ledger was introduced. This gives details of every employee and the wages paid to them from 1st January, 1894 to 31st December, 1943. As head of the business Charley Holdroyd is not included in the list; each page to the end of March 1913 is headed by his youngest brother, George Henry Holdroyd. There are some familiar names listed as some of the employees lived at Upper Banks or Banks, but employment opportunities were changing for the residents of Honley.

From at least 1881 to 1901 Hamer Bray's neighbour at number 18 Far Banks was George Orson Chambers. In 1891, George was a woollen weaver, however the 1901 census indicates that he had found employment in a new area. Although he was 68 years of age, his occupation was shown to be that of lamplighter for the council - a reflection of the innovations of the time and the ever improving services and utilities. The gas works had been established some years earlier and were sited at Honley Bridge, at the bottom of the Old Turnpike on land leased to the company by the Earl of Dartmouth.

The new development was not without its difficulties, being viewed with suspicion and fear by many people in the village. This was probably justified as an explosion there on 4th July, 1899 resulted in four men losing their lives. There is a comprehensive account of the introduction of both gas and electricity to the village, as well as the work to bring piped water into the area, in the Civic Society's publication *Honley Bridge and Newtown*.[14]

A young Charley Holdroyd in an undated studio photograph

John William Holdroyd, still of Quarry House, the eldest of Edward's sons, died on 30th May, 1897 aged 59 years. Effects were valued at £373 1s 6d, with probate granted to his widow, Edna, and to sons John Edward Holdroyd, a Co-operative stores manager and Arthur Holdroyd, an insurance agent.

A later legal document makes reference to a historical agreement dated 5th October, 1897 between (1) Joseph Green and (2) Emily Charlotte Carter, (3) Hamer Bray, (4) Lavinia Ann Bray, (5) Fred Sharp, (6) William Bray, (7) Hannah Maria Clarkson, Helen Tilburn & Ruth Billcliffe, (8) Ruth Hannah Hinchliffe & Sarah Ellen Buckley, (9) Sarah Ann Bray & Ruth Hannah Barker, (10) David Kinder and (11) Charley Holdroyd. Although it later related to 10 Banks, in 1897 it actually concerned the adjoining properties, namely the row of cottages (numbers 2 to 8) and the old joinery workshop. The cottages were now surrounded by the joinery business and Charley Holdroyd may have felt that he needed to have ownership of them to allow greater flexibility in terms of the use of land which he planned to develop. It is likely that a key part of his development plan was the construction of a larger house adjoining number 8 and its inevitable impact on access to the rear of all the properties.

The 1897 agreement involved many more people than could have been living in the cottages. The involvement of members of the Bray family is clear. In 1897 siblings Lavinia and Hamer were still living at numbers 8 and 16 respectively. However the other names appeared initially to be without connection, it was only sight of the original Indenture that clarified the individual interests in the cottages.

In addition to properties at Upper Banks, the cottages that would later become numbers 2, 6 and 8 as well as other buildings nearby appear to have originally belonged to John Bray, a cloth miller of Meal Hill, Bank End. As noted, the 1838 map shows the bank at the rear of the houses to have been known as the Meal Hill and the 1841 census shows John and his wife Grace to be at number 16, the first and maybe largest property on Upper Banks.

John Bray died on 15th July, 1853 and his will was proven in the Prerogatives Court in York by his executors, sons Benjamin and John Levi and his son-in-law, George Sharpe. In his will dated 9th January, 1853 he left all his property in trust for his 'dearly beloved wife, Grace', for the duration of her life. Thereafter his real estate was to be divided amongst his seven surviving children, Sarah Ann, Lavinia Ann, Benjamin Townend, Eliza, Michael, Hamer and John Levi. An added contingency was that, in the event of their deaths, an individual's share should be divided between their 'legitimate or illegitimate issue'.

The 1897 agreement to sell the properties was drawn up 45 years after John Bray's death so, as may be expected, several of his children and even grandchildren, had already died. This means that, with a couple of exceptions, the people named in the document are the children, grandchildren and great-grandchildren of John Bray. Emily Carter was Michael Bray's daughter. Fred Sharp, who was Eliza's child, and William Bray, son of John Levi Bray were John Bray's grandsons. Hannah Clarkson, Helen Tilburn and Ruth Billcliffe were the daughters of Benjamin Townend Bray, whilst Ruth Hinchliffe, Sarah Buckley, Sarah Bray and Ruth Barker were Benjamin's grandchildren. Joseph Green, a retired mill manager living on Co-operative Terrace, Honley, was a friend of Michael Bray and had been appointed as his executor and trustee. David Kinder, a saddler from Honley Bridge, had been similarly appointed by Benjamin.

Tea Urn presented to Charley and Emma Holdroyd
on their silver wedding anniversary in January 1899

The agreement related to 'all those three cottages or dwelling houses with outbuildings and conveniences thereto belonging and a plot of vacant land adjoining occupied therewith, situate at Banks Honley'. The properties are noted to be 'now in the occupation of Mrs Wright Jillott, Allan Jillott and Mrs F Roodhouse'. The second property was initially harder to identify. The indenture refers to 'all that cottage or dwelling house with the shops underneath, the same outbuildings and conveniences thereto belonging, and vacant land adjoining occupied therewith, situate at Banks Honley'.

This property is confirmed as being in the occupation of Hamer Bray. This second property probably refers to number 16, as we know that this is where he was living. Whilst most of the properties on Upper Banks were at a higher level, number 16 was the only one adjacent to the road. It seems to have been a shop or workshop at road level with the dwelling house above it. It isn't clear but, given that Holdroyds are later known to have also owned the wooded slope between Banks and the Woodhead Road and the woodland stretching from the road down to the river, this may also have been part of this transaction, perhaps constituting the 'vacant lands adjoining'.

Charley Holdroyd paid £360 for the land and the cottages. He would have bought them for the business thereby ensuring a regular income from the rent they would bring in. A later tax document shows him to now be the recipient of rents on the properties at numbers 2, 8 and 16. However, and maybe of more significance, he now owned more of the Banks land and the buildings on it.

It is apparent from the legal documents that the person who received the income from the remainder of the land at Banks was Emma Hoyle, nee Middleton, that is, all that had not been previously acquired from Joe Jessop by the Holdroyds or was part of Charley Holdroyd's growing property portfolio. The Middleton holdings still included the land and possibly also the offices, workshops and warehouses on it that were part of Edward Holdroyd & Sons.

It also included the dwelling house that Edwin Holdroyd's widow was still living in and an area of land adjacent to it. The Middletons also owned much of the land that was occupied by the dwellings at Upper Banks. Walter Middleton's will had directed that his wife, Ann Middleton, was to have 'use of rents' during her life. Thereafter the rents were to go to his daughter, Emma Hoyle, 'during her life for her separate use and after her decease testator directed that his trustees should sell the said hereditaments either by public auction or private contract and the family stand possessed of the proceeds'.

Ann Middleton had died in May 1891. Her eldest son, John Middleton, died in June 1897, leaving his younger brother, Walter Middleton (junior), as sole trustee. His sister, Emma Hoyle, was now living with her husband and their five remaining children in Liscard, Birkenhead. Of their eight children, Percy had died in 1889 aged 11 and, more recently, the couple had lost Arthur (junior) aged ten and Hervin aged 18. With many demands on their attention, the Hoyles were evidently keen to hand over some of the property at Banks to new owners rather than wait for Emma's death as her father's will had stipulated.

An Indenture dated 27th October, 1899, between Emma Hoyle, Arthur Hoyle, Walter Middleton Hoyle and Maria Turner, states that, 'All the interest of the said Emma Hoyle of and in the hereditaments and premises comprised in the said will of the said Walter Middleton was conveyed and assigned by the said Emma Hoyle unto the said Maria Turner by way of Mortgage to secure payment of the sum of sixty pounds with interest thereon'. There is little to indicate what this relates to, but it suggests that Emma, with the agreement of her husband and son had put all her interests in the property into the hands of Maria Turner, who had then conveyed them to John Edward Heap, solicitor of Gynn View Villas, Honley. With no record to confirm who Maria Turner was, we cannot determine if she was a relative of the Hoyles, an associate or employee of John Heap or connected to the Turners who are later identified as 'Agents', based at Station Road, Holmfirth.

So, at the end of the century, some of the land and property at Banks was still in the ownership of the Middleton family, but rented to the Holdroyds. It is clear however that, having now bought the cottages and the land surrounding them, Charley Holdroyd would have had his eye on acquiring the remaining buildings and land that were actually used by his joinery business.

Sarah Louise North.

BANKS: 1900 TO 1904

Within the Banks community, everyone would have known their neighbours and property numbering would not have been necessary to identify where people lived. This had changed by the time of the 1901 census which shows Sarah-Ann Holdroyd, now a 59-year-old widow, living at 14 Banks, with eight of her children, aged between 29 and 14. Only Frank, aged 22, is shown to be working as a carpenter and joiner. The official address of Edward Holdroyd & Sons might have been 12 Banks, but this was never used. Lavinia Bray was still sharing her home at number 8 with Allen and Edna Jillott and their family. A railway labourer, John Wood, was at number 2 with his wife Caroline and their 10-year-old son Henry. Charley and Emma Holdroyd were now officially recorded as living at 4 Banks, but their eldest son Harry and his new wife, Sarah Louise, had moved into a larger and newly built house at number 10.

Five years earlier, in 1896, Harry Holdroyd, then aged 21 years, had travelled via Liverpool and Ireland to Boston, Massachusetts, USA. Records show that he sailed on the *SS Pavonia* arriving on 25th October, as a visitor. A month later, he returned from New York, on the *RMS Campania*, to arrive back in Liverpool on 27th November. On both trips, his occupation is shown as architect. He also appears to have travelled alone.[1] Even within the family there was no such thing as 'holiday pay'. Harry's absence from work during this time is marked in the ledger with dashes, indicating that no wage was paid to him.

Sarah Louise North (known to her family as Sadie) was born in 1870 in Providence, Rhode Island, USA, and lived in Woonsocket, close to the Massachusetts border and not far from Boston. A history website for New England families shows that Sarah North and Harry Holdroyd were married in Woonsocket on 11th June, 1900, very soon after a census was taken in that area.[15] The census shows that her father, John North, was born in England in 1844. This is confirmed in the 1851 and 1861 UK censuses, which show him to be in Honley. John's parents were Thomas North and Hannah Holroyd (sic), evidence that the families were probably related. After Thomas died, Hannah remarried and John and his sister, also Sarah, both appear on the 1861 census as Joseph Goldthorpe's step-children. Soon after this John evidently went to the US, marrying Sarah Elizabeth Bentley. Sarah Louise was the second of their seven children. Following their marriage, Harry Holdroyd brought 'American Sarah' to live in Honley.

The wages ledger indicates that Harry and Sarah Holdroyd returned to Honley in September. He does not appear on the electoral register for 1900, but they are both recorded on the 1901 census which was taken on 31st March. This records them living at 10 Banks. The 1902 electoral register shows that Harry had already given the new house at number 10 a name - Boston Cottage. This was doubtless done in recognition of a place that was special to them both.

Nellie Holdroyd at No.4 Banks with Hope Bank in background

Nellie in the garden of No.4 Banks

Harold North Holdroyd with his Auntie Nellie

Birth entry for Harold North

1902							
July 10th No. 43	August 20th	Harold North	Harry & Sarah Louise	Holdroyd	Honley	Joiner	G.A. Stoke curate

Sarah's sister, Selina, who was ten years her junior, is recorded as being in Honley from May to October 1902 [15]. She is likely to have come to stay to help Sarah through a first pregnancy and would therefore have been with the family when Sarah died on 24th July, 1902, six days after giving birth to a son, Harold North Holdroyd. Sarah's gravestone is in Honley, but there is also another for her in Rhode Island. Both show the family name for her of 'Sadie'.

John North visited Honley soon after this sad event. He then returned to the US in October 1902 accompanied by Harry's sister, Ellen (Nellie) Holdroyd, who was then aged 23. They travelled from Liverpool to Boston on the *SS New England*. Her occupation is given as a servant, but there are also separate notes stating that she and John North are both friends and cousins. Travel records indicate that they were both headed for Woonsocket, Rhode Island.[1] Nellie evidently stayed there for several weeks before being joined by her younger brother Norman in December. Maybe he had been sent to escort her home as they then returned together on the *SS Ivernia*, the same ship Norman had sailed out on, arriving back in Liverpool in January 1903. The families were doubtless united in their grief at the loss of Sarah, but there were also developments in the joinery business that required attention.

A few weeks earlier, an Indenture, dated 4th December, 1902, between Walter Middleton and Joe Middleton (the late John Middleton's son, who was now 21 years old) had identified Joe as having been appointed co-trustee of his grandfather's will. This preceded other documents relating to their apparent decision, along with Emma Hoyle, to sell their real estate at Banks. A large part of this property comprised the joiners shop, garage, outbuildings and adjoining land being used in the occupation of Edward Holdroyd & Sons, Joiners and Contractors.

Unsurprisingly, this property was bought by Charley Holdroyd. Reference is made to the conveyance, dated 24th February, 1903, between (1) Emma Hoyle, (2) John Edward Heap, (3) Walter Middleton and Joe Middleton and (4) Charley Holdroyd. Also, documents relating to the imminent sale of the remaining land refer to 'hereditaments ... on the northwestwardly side ... previously owned by Walter and Joe Middleton, but lately sold to Charley Holdroyd'. John Heap, of Sykes, Heap, Marshall and Healy, was the solicitor employed to oversee the conveyance process.

In respect of the area at the southern end of Banks, Emma Hoyle and Walter and Joe Middleton put this part of the property up for sale by auction on the 2nd January, 1903. The property comprised the dwelling house at 14 Banks and an area of land to the south of it. The total area of the land being sold was 1,275 square yards. The auction took place at the Wheatsheaf (sometimes Wheat Sheaf) Inn in Honley.

The inn, at 15 Southgate (formerly Far End Lane), was run by Esther Heap, John Heap's mother. The 1901 census recorded her as a 64-year-old widow. Of her four daughters who shared her home, three were assistant innkeepers and one, Sarah, was an Assistant Teacher at the National school. There are a couple of references to Miss Sarah Heap in the Honley Civic Society's publication, *Honley National School 1816 – 1952*.[16] The book does not, however, record that Miss Heap's mother ran a local pub!

At the auction on 2nd January, 1903, 'Lot 1' comprised 'a plot of land on ground situate at Banks, Honley (formerly part of a close of land called the Meal Hill)'. This contained an area of '1,275 superficial square yards'. Documents refer to the messuage, that is, the house and the buildings assigned to its use. Clarification of the proposed sale is offered as being of unto and to the use of the said Esther Heap her heirs and assigns for ever And the said Esther Heap hereby covenants with the said Emma Hoyle that she the said Esther Heap her heirs or assigns will forthwith fence off to the satisfaction of the said Emma Hoyle the hereditaments hereby conveyed from the hereditaments adjoining on the North westwardly side thereof as indicated by the marks TT on the said plan _Provided always_ that as regards the remainder or expectant on the estate for life of the said Emma Hoyle in the hereditaments hereby conveyed her covenants for title implied by law shall not extend to the acts or defaults of any person other than and besides herself and persons claiming or to claim under or in trust for her _And_ the said Walter Middleton (party hereto) and Joe Middleton hereby acknowledge the right of the said Esther Heap to production of the herein before recited Indenture of the fourth day of December one thousand nine hundred and two and to delivery of copies thereof _In Witness_ whereof the said parties to these presents have hereunto set their hands and seals the day and year first herein before written

Signed Sealed and Delivered
by the said Emma Hoyle in the
presence of C. W. Marshall   Emma Hoyle   [seal]

        Wk. Sclispild   J. E. Heap   [seal]

Signed sealed and delivered by the   Walter Middleton   [seal]
said John Edward Heap Walter Middleton
and Joe Middleton in the presence of   Joe Middleton   [seal]
        Arthur Heap
   Clerk to Sykes Heap Marshall & Hedley   Esther Heap   [seal]
        Solicitors Huddersfield.

Signed sealed and delivered by the
said Esther Heap in the presence of
        Thomas Anson
        Church St
        Honley

        A Copy of this Indenture was registered at the
        West Riding Registry of Deeds at Wakefield the
        twenty sixth of February 1903 at 2.45 in the
        afternoon in Volume 9 Page 341 Number
                    J. W. Snyden Registrar.

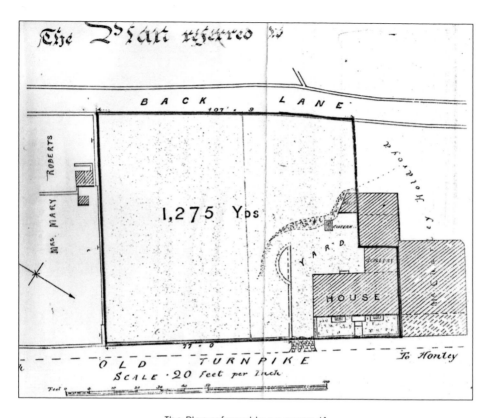

The Plan referred to on page 41

The extract from the Indenture relating to the sale of Banks House in 1903 (*opposite*) shows a little of how the documents were written, highlighting the small, close handwriting and the complete absence of punctuation.

The signatures on the right alongside the seals are those of (*from top to bottom*)

Emma Hoyle, John Edward Heap, Walter Middleton, Joe Middleton, Esther Heap

Signed, sealed and delivered in the presence of representatives of Sykes, Heap, Marshall & Healey, Solicitors, Holmfirth.

Signed sealed and delivered by the said Esther Heap in the presence of Thomas Avison Church St Honley.

The stamp at the foot of the document reads: A copy of this Indenture was registered at the West Riding Registry of Deeds at Wakefield the twenty sixth of February 1903 at 2.45 in the afternoon in Volume 9 page 341 Number 169

The Wheatsheaf Inn, Far End Lane later called Southgate

Looking northwards on Southgate, with the Inn in the middle distance on the right. The large property on the right, once Taylor and Jones is now a dwelling house at the entrance to Southgate Fold

the dwelling house, scullery and outbuildings, together with the right in common with others to fetch water from the domestic pump'. Also, right to lights overhanging, chimneys, drains etc and 'other privileges in the nature of easements in common with adjoining property comprising Lot 2'.

Whilst we don't officially know what Lot 2 comprised, the term 'adjoining' indicates that it includes the workshop as well as other parts of the wider Banks property, occupied by Edward Holdroyd & Sons. This is especially likely given that information suggests that it was all bought by Charley Holdroyd.

A map, or 'The Plan referred to' (*page 39*), shows the Lot 1 area to comprise that which now covers Banks House, its outbuildings and the land above it immediately to the south. The land beyond this is shown as being owned by Mrs Mary Roberts. Mary is likely to have been the widowed daughter of John Haigh, coal merchant from Hall Ing, and one of the former owners of Banks Mill and its surrounding land. The land to the north, incorporating the joinery buildings is shown to be already owned by Charley Holdroyd. A complete copy of this plan may be found in Appendix 2.

At the rear of the house is a scullery, indicating that the kitchen with the bathroom above it was yet to be added. The end part of the building across the yard is marked as a 'privy', with a cistern nearby. The 'bank' has been included, illustrating the elevation of most of the land in relation to the house. The identification of the road outside as the Old Turnpike suggests the use of an old map.

It seems surprising that Charley Holdroyd did not buy Lot 1 to complete his ownership of Banks. Maybe he tried, but at the auction Esther Heap was noted to have been the highest bidder and was declared to be the purchaser at a price of £354. An Indenture, dated 21st February, 1903, between Maria Turner and John Edward Heap seems to relate to the conveying of monies ahead of the actual property transfer.

On 24th February, 1903, an Indenture was completed between (1) Emma Hoyle, (2) John Edward Heap, (3) Walter Middleton & Joe Middleton and (4) Esther Heap. Esther Heap having been declared the purchaser, £354 was paid to Emma Hoyle as per the will directive and under the Settled Land Acts 1882 and 1890. There was also a note of consent to John E Heap being party to the conveyance. John, as Esther's son, had doubtless advised his widowed mother on the wisdom of acquiring property that would bring her an additional income. The note of consent might have been to avoid any issues about a possible conflict of interest. The Indenture, prepared by Sykes, Heap, Marshall & Healey, Solicitors, confirmed the property transfer and that Esther Heap was now the owner of what would later be known as Banks House, as well as the adjacent land.

An advertisement for Holdroyds

BANKS: 1904 TO 1910

B y 1904, Edward Holdroyd and Sons, under the management of Charley Holdroyd, owned all the properties at Banks, with the exception of the dwelling house at number 14 and its associated land which had been bought by Esther Heap. Charley was now evidently keen to promote his business as much as possible.

The range of services and goods (*opposite*) is impressive, if a little incomprehensible! The flexibility of the business is summarised in the statement that Holdroyd's provide 'All kinds of Jobbing Work Promptly and Carefully Executed'.

The receipt illustrated on the page 47 contains a stylised and somewhat too perfect graphic of Banks. Artistic licence has suggested space, light and cleanliness where all would have been limited. Such licence is also evident in the statement that Holdroyds had been established for over a century, although the date line is printed to accept a 1900s year. The business is generally recorded as having begun in 1817, however, Edward's father, the first John Holdroyd, had already been a joiner at the time of his son's birth in 1817 so Charley's reasoning was probably sound. Assuming John was born during the early 1790s, he may well have been working from a relatively early age and, as noted earlier, maybe his own father was a joiner too, in which case the Holdroyd's joinery business may date from even further back. The handwritten notes on the receipt were later added by Charley's grandson.

As the advertisement and receipt both show, Edward Holdroyd & Sons were connected to the telephone network earlier than many businesses would have been. Directories had existed from 1880, although information in them was limited. The *Ancestry* website provides many old directory records, including that for 1897 – 1898, which shows the entry as:

Honley 6   HOLDROYD   E. & Sons .... Banks, Honley

Their phone number was Honley 6, which was later also used for the family at Boston Cottage via an extension, thereby providing 24-hour contact. It is likely that this number was still in use as late as 1958 when the introduction of Subscriber Trunk Dialling, the facility to make calls without the services of an operator, changed the number to Honley 61306.

On 19th May, 1904, Harry Holdroyd married his second wife, Mary Annie Lancaster. A wedding photograph (*page 44*) shows the Holdroyd family in all their finery at the reception which was held at Mytholmbridge House in Thongsbridge.

It's probable that the often published photograph of the Holdroyds' workforce [17] (*page 46 top*)was taken in 1905, maybe even to celebrate the expansion of the business. The workers are positioned outside the offices and workshops of Edward Holdroyd and Sons, with members of the Holdroyd family outside number 10 Banks. The picture shows Charley and Harry Holdroyd, together with Mary Annie, who is holding her new baby. Marion Beatrice, born 6th April, 1905, would always be known as Beatrice, or Bea. The small boy is Harold North Holdroyd, holding onto the hand of his father, Harry.

Newly married couple, Harry and Mary, (left), Charley and Emma Letitia are seated with grandchildren Charles Leslie and Harold North. Standing behind are Charles' parents Evelyn and Lewis, with Nellie and Norman (*right*).

Charley and Emma Letitia Holdroyd outside their home at 4 Banks with grandson Harold North Holdroyd

Number 10 is yet to have its columns added; timber can be seen stacked in the yard just beyond number 2 and number 14 – just visible in the lower left corner – still has the railings that would eventually be sacrificed for the war effort. The second photograph appears to have been taken at the same time and shows some of the other residents of Banks.

In June 1908, in another change to the management structure of Holdroyds, it appears that Harry Holdroyd may have joined his father to become joint owner or partner in the business. Having been on the list of employees from the start of the Holdroyd's wages ledger in 1894, his name suddenly disappears from it altogether. Other family members are consistent in their positions within the firm, specifically Charley's youngest brother, George Henry, and Harry's brothers Lewis and Norman. Also of note is Beatrice's 1905 birth registration record, where Harry's occupation is shown as builder, indicating that the business had expanded from the joinery that it started out as.

By this time changes had also taken place in the occupancy of the house at 14 Banks. It is assumed that Esther Heap had bought the house in 1903 to rent out, with Edwin Holdroyd's widow, Sarah, as the sitting tenant. However, Sarah died in June 1904 aged 63. From this time, whilst most of the Banks properties enjoyed long term occupancy, number 14 would change hands on numerous occasions.

The electoral registers for 1904 to 1906 show 14 Banks to be occupied by George Beaumont Gledhill. In 1901 George had been living with his three sisters at Highfield House on Eastgate. Then aged 24, he was a bobbin manufacturer, as his father had been ten years earlier, probably running Gledhill and Roberts at the Bridge Bobbin Works [19]. George moved to Marsh Platt, off Gynn Lane, in 1907 and married Kate Wimpenny the following year.

It is likely that the extension to the house was completed following George Gledhill's departure. The scullery was replaced with a kitchen, and a bathroom was installed above it. The kitchen having a lower ceiling than other ground floor rooms meant that access to the bathroom above required two steps down to it as well as being through a 20 inch thick wall. Other changes that may date from this time are the boarding up of a door into the original scullery and two new doorways to access the new kitchen via a lobby. This meant difficulties in accessing the cellar had to be addressed by extending the floor and leaving the first step down to be double its previous height.

From 1909 to 1913, records show that the house was occupied by Joseph Hall, although he may actually have been there from 1907. Joseph was resident at the property at the time of the 1911 census. This shows him as a 37-year-old commercial traveller and woollen merchant, originally from Golcar. He was living with his 30-year-old wife, Daisy Ethel Pyle Hall, whom he had married in Chorlton, Manchester in the summer of 1905. They had a 3-year-old son, John, and employed a 20-year-old general servant (domestic) named Lucy Burks.

Some confusion (and, it must be acknowledged, intrigue) arose when, from 1910, Daisy was noted to be also renting the cottage at number 2 from Charley Holdroyd. However, this was explained by the 1911 census that showed the property to be occupied by Margaret Bailey and earlier records from the 1881 census, which clarified that Margaret was Daisy Ethel Pyle Bailey's mother, who had evidently relocated from Middlesbrough to be near to her daughter.

The workforce outside the offices and workshops of Edward Holdroyd and Sons, with members of the Holdroyd family outside number 10 Banks ,

Family members, *from left to right* are:- Harold North Holdroyd holding the hand of his father, Harry Holdroyd, Mary Annie Holdroyd with her father in law, Charley Holdroyd, outside number 10; Charley is holding his new grand-daughter, Beatrice Holdroyd, The lady in the doorway of number 8 may be Hannah Jillott and the ladies furthest away, standing in front of number 4, are probably Emma Letitia Holdroyd, Lavinia Bray and Nellie Holdroyd.

The image of Holdrody's works may be somewhat exaggerated but would have been created to give a good impression. The handwritten notes on the receipt were later added by Charley's grandson.

Holdroyd's woodyard

55

No. of Assessment	No. of Poor Rate.	Christian Names and Surnames of Occupiers.	Christian Names and Surnames of Owners, with their Residences.	Description of Property—If an Inn, &c., the name or sign by which known.	No. of House.	Street, Place, Name, and Precise Situation of Property.	Poor Rate.					Reference to Map.
							Estimated Extent.		Gross Annual Value.		Rateable Value.	
1	2	3	4	5		6	7		8		9	11
							Acres.	R.	£	s.	£	s.
1/010	90be	Ed Holdroyd & Sons	Earl Dartmouth	Land ✓		Hagg Leys	5	½0	6 15		6 4	
1	7	Harry Holdroyd	Charley Holdroyd & Banks	Houses	10	Boston Cottage			18		15	
2	8	Allen Jillott	"	House	8	Banks			5		3 16	
3	9	Charley Holdroyd	"	"	44	"			13 5		10	
4	910	Daisy Ethel Hall	"	"	2	"			4 5		3 4	

The 1910 tax record shows the significance of the Jillott family
to the Banks story.

The gravestone of the Jillott family in Honley graveyard

In Affectionate Remembrance of
FRED
SON OF ALLEN & EDNA JILLOTT
OF HONLEY
WHO DIED MAY 23RD 1883
AGED 3 YEARS
ALSO ELLEN ANN *THEIR DAUGHTER*
WHO DIED MARCH 24TH 1885
AGED 2 YEARS
ALSO EDNA *WIFE OF* ALLEN JILLOTT
WHO DIED SEPTEMBER 17TH 1895
AGED 50 YEARS
ALSO OF ALLEN JILLOTT
WHO DIED SEPTEMBER 6TH 1910
AGED 62 YEARS
ALSO OF SARAH *DAUGHTER*
OF THE ABOVE
WHO DIED OCT 23RD 1911
AGED 32 YEARS

The 1910 tax record shows the value of the properties at 2 to 10 Banks, and also answers the question of why number 6 disappears from the records for a significant period of time. It seems that, his father having already doubled the size of the property in the 1850s, Charley Holdroyd and his family had now also joined numbers 4 and 6 together; the properties having been linked by connecting doors on both floors. These alterations probably took place around 1895.

Another observation from this record is that Edward Holdroyd & Sons also paid rent on five acres of land at Hagg Leys, where Far Banks meets the Oldfield Road at Upper Hagg. Rents were payable to the Earl of Dartmouth, who is known to have owned large areas of land in the region, having his country seat at Blake Lea House in Marsden. In her book on the history of nearby Farnley Tyas, Caroline Page notes that much of the surrounding area was once part of the Earl of Dartmouth's estate. 'Lord Dartmouth's Yorkshire Estates originally included Farnley Tyas, part of Thurstonland, Brockholes, Honley, Meltham, Almondbury, Lepton, Kirkburton, Slaithwaite and Morley'.[20] The Earl evidently took a keen interest in the life of Honley village and is acknowledged as a significant supporter and benefactor in a number of the Honley Civic Society's publications.

Also shown in the ledger and of significance to the Banks story is the Jillott family. In 1841 Lydia Jillott was at 24 Upper Banks, surrounded by Brays. In 1851, Hannah and Thomas Jillott were living at Woodnook; where son Allen was aged 3 years. Following his marriage in October 1876 to Edna Bray, Allen had moved to live with her family on Upper Banks. By 1881, it is clear that this actually refers to number 8 Banks, the home of Lavinia Ann Bray, Edna's mother. By 1891 they had been joined by his brother, Wright, who had married Sarah Carter in December 1880, and who lived at number 6 until 1895. Lavinia and her brother Hamer Bray were signatories to the agreement relating to the sale of the cottages to Charley Holdroyd in 1897.

Edna Jillott had died in 1895, aged 50. Her uncle Hamer Bray died in May 1902 aged 80, and her mother Lavinia died in 1908, aged 93. Lavinia appears to have never married; Edna's 1845 birth has no father recorded. This may have prompted the inclusion of the line in her grandfather's 1853 will relating to 'legitimate or illegitimate issue'. After Allen Jillott's death in 1910, his daughter Hannah remained at number 8, to be joined by her sister Emily in 1928. Hannah died in 1950, but Emily was at the house until 1966. Thomas Jillott, son of Wright and Sarah, moved into number 2 Banks in 1918, marrying Sarah Jane Lancashire in August 1919. The couple were still at the house when Thomas died in March 1972. Sarah left Banks in 1974 and died in March 1982 aged 86.

Since the 1841 census shows several Brays, Lydia Jillott and John and Grace Holdroyd at Upper Banks, the families all share the record for at least 120 years residence at Banks.

The newly built Sunny Bank with attention being given to the roadway in front.

The northern end of Far Banks in 2018

BANKS: FAR BANKS
AND THE 1911 CENSUS

Dates are approximate but sometime between 1904 and 1907, the terrace of five houses appeared at Far Banks, just beyond Upper Banks. Like the properties that would follow them along Far Banks and through Upper Hagg, they were built by Edward Holdroyd & Sons. The houses at Upper Banks were numbered from 16 to 38, so the new houses became 40 to 48. Four of these four-storey properties have stone steps running sideways up to the front doors, the fifth is set at 90 degrees and has a larger garden. This one, number 48, is called Sunny Bank.

By 1911, all five properties were occupied generally by people with higher positions of responsibility in their employment. The 1911 census shows that Richard Whittaker, a commercial traveller and his family were at number 40. Brook Lancaster, a cloth finisher and dyer, and his wife Edith, were at number 42 and Norman Hague Hope, a woollen and worsted manufacturer and his wife Charlotte were at 44. Harry Marsden, manager of the gas and electricity works was at number 46 with his wife, Laura, and at number 48, Sunny Bank, was builder and joiner Norman Holdroyd and his wife Amy (nee France), whom he had married in December 1907. A short distance away, Norman's older brother Lewis and his wife Evelyn (nee Gledhill) were living at 8 Hagg Leys. To mark an event as auspicious as the ten-yearly census, their nine-year-old son, (Charles) Leslie, had evidently been allowed to write his own name on the census form!

The 1910 tax record shows that whilst Norman Holdroyd owned number 48, the other four houses at Far Banks still belonged to their builder, Harry Holdroyd. He also still owned number 16, which was now occupied by Joe Sykes. Joseph Hall is recorded as occupying number 14 Banks with property ownership still assigned to Esther Heap. However, her name has then been crossed out and replaced, in a different ink, with that of Ronald Butterworth. It is not clear whether this name was added later or if he had bought the house from her with Joseph Hall as the sitting tenant. The houses at Upper Banks, numbered 18 to 38, remained in the possession of the executors of the late Walter Middleton. With the Hoyles living on the Wirral, the rents must have been collected for them by a third party. Perhaps the fact that the Hoyles were, effectively, absentee landlords might explain the slow decline in these properties that would be apparent over the following years.

As Honley expanded more new properties were also built around the same time, extending Far Banks towards Upper Hagg. Wood View and Far Bank came first, having already been built sometime between 1894 and 1902. They appear, in dramatic isolation, in a photograph (*page 54*) looking across the Pleasure Ground from the hill above Brockholes.

The Mount (referred to initially and on some maps as The Mound) appeared in 1910, Hillcrest and the properties beyond all appeared during the 1920s. One of these, Raymount, at number 80 has a date on it of 1929 and houses at Upper Hagg were built around 1932, so progress was relatively swift. The two semi-detached houses Norwood and Glen Dene, now numbered 54 and 56 Far Banks, appeared around 1939.

The best known picture to show any part of the original houses at Upper Banks.
They can be seen, in their elevated position, behind the new terraced houses at
Far Banks. On the picture of Sunny Bank, the chimney on the right is probably at
Crossley Mills. Close inspection also shows a chimney at the very left of the picture;
this must be the one that the receipt graphic above indicates existed at Holdroyds.

Far Bank from the south

The 1911 census records the people living in the earlier-built of these properties. Wood View is a pair of semi detached houses; at the first one reached from Banks was Charles Ernest Thornton, his wife, Mary and their family. He was a foreman in the woollen worsted cloth dyeing business. Mary died in 1954, but Charles was at Wood View until 1963. His 1911 neighbour was Robert Oliver Pott, a textile designer, also in woollen worsted cloth, whose eldest son was his assistant. At Far Bank, Oswald Hirst Sykes was a cloth manufacturer and at The Mount, was Herbert Samuel Drake, a corn miller. All are recorded as employers of a workforce and all four of the families at these properties had the support of at least one member of household staff.

In the other direction from Banks, towards the village centre, the records show that Kate Jessop, Joe Jessop's widow, was still at 1 Ryecroft. Aged 58, she was living by 'private means'. 3 Ryecroft, previously occupied by the Thornton family, was now the home of Wesleyan Methodist Minister, Rev Henry Allen Rigall and his wife Mary, aged 32 and 27 respectively. At 5 Ryecroft was 29-year-old local medical practitioner, Dr William Herbert Smailes and his wife Hilda. Again, all three households benefitted from the support of paid staff. Behind Ryecroft, where Far End Lane meets Field End Lane, Tom Allen Thornton and his family were now at George Brookes' old house Fern Leigh.

Returning to Banks and the 1911 census shows Charley and Emma Holdroyd still at number 4. Daughter Ellen (always known as Nellie), now 32, was unmarried and still living with them. They also had a servant, Florence Green. Harry and Mary were at 10 Banks with their two children, Harold North, now eight-years-old, and (Marion) Beatrice, aged six. They too had live-in domestic help from 19-year-old Emma Brown. Harry may by now have added the two stone carvings of Lord Kitchener on either side of the front door, above which he had earlier carved the date 1900 and the name Boston Cottage, presumably to mark the date the house was built and to acknowledge the place that that had connections to his first wife. However, the columns would not be added for several more years.

Far Banks from Sunny Bank (number 48) in 2018

The focus of the photographer was on the splendid 1910 Renault 7 that apparently belonged to Harry Holdroyd and which survives to the present day. We can also see one of the original houses at Upper Banks at the end of Far Banks. The house is number 38, with number 16 behind it, as this was above a workshop that was at road level.

As Honley expanded more new properties were also built around the same time, extending Far towards Upper Hagg. Wood View and Far Bank came first, having already been built sometime between 1894 and 1902. They appear, in dramatic isolation, across the Pleasure Ground from Brockholes.

BANKS: 1911 – 1918
AND THE GREAT WAR

Whilst Edward Holdroyd and Sons seems to have provided a relatively stable environment in which to work, the wages ledger for 1911 gives up a story of a possible 'summer of discontent' amongst the apprentices. A slip of paper in the book contains a letter that reads, 'Sir, We your apprentices feel the wages we receive are not sufficient for our maintenance ... We therefore ask for an advance of one half'. The four men have each signed the letter, including a figure stating what they feel to be due to them. Perhaps fearing that they may have been too deferential, they then conclude with a note that 'Work stops Thursday evening if no answer'. In response, the ledger for August details a review of apprentice pay and the agreement to pay the 'advanced wage' requested.

Despite the loss of his daughter, John North had evidently maintained contact with his Honley roots, with the Holdroyd family in England and especially with his grandson. John died in 1914, aged 70, whilst on a visit and was, as a consequence, buried in Honley cemetery. On Ed Hamilton's *New England Families* website, it is noted that most members of the North family were buried in Oak Hill Cemetery, Woonsocket, but that Sarah's mother's grave bears an inscription that reads, 'John North died on 22nd August, 1914 and is buried in Honley, England' [15]. Similarly, Sarah (Sadie) had her name added to the grave of her older sister, Hannah. Photographs of the graves are shown on page 58.

In 1914, Mary Jagger's *The History of Honley* [3] was published. She lived at 46 Southgate, the only brick-built house in the area. Her book covers the history of the village and gives considerable detail that is current to her time. In doing so, she would have been referring to people who were living at the time of publication. There are a couple of references to the Holdroyds, including Harry's name appearing on a list of current councillors for the Honley South Ward, a role that had previously been held by his father, Charley.

In chapter five of *The History of Honley*, a paragraph headed, *Various Trades of Honley* includes the following:

> *The Holdroyd family have sustained an unbroken record of over 100 years in the trade of joiners of high local standing. Their forefathers were noted for making good articles of household furniture which were handed down as heirlooms. Honley's old-time manufacturers made cloth with the intention of never wearing out, so the furniture constructed by the Holdroyds of a past day was put together on the same principle. The present members of the family have upheld the reputation for high-class workmanship as of old, whilst also keeping abreast with modern requirements and rapid changes.* [3]

There is a further reference to the work of the Holdroyds in Honley Civic Society's publication, *Honley National School 1816 – 1952*,[17] which notes that work to enlarge the school to meet the requirements of the 1870 Education Act, was undertaken by local contractors. The list includes 'joinery by Edward Holdroyd of Far Banks, Honley'. Later, a 1901 expansion of the school records that the 'desks were made locally by Charley Holdroyd of Far Banks'.[16]

John North with his grandson, Harold North Holdroyd,
in 1907 when the boy was five-years-old

In addition to sitting on the local council, both Charley and Harry Holdroyd were members of the Holme Valley Masonic Lodge. They appear on a register of members from which we see that Charley Holdroyd, joiner & builder, joined in March 1892 and that Harry Holdroyd became a member in November 1898. Other local Masons were gas manager Harry Marsden and commercial traveller Joseph Hall, who joined in April 1906 and March 1910 respectively. From January 1899 John Edward Heap was also a member, joining his co-partners in Sykes, Heap, Marshall and Heeley Solicitors. [22]

The electoral register for 1914 shows that Joseph and Daisy Hall had moved on, being found later to be living in Berry Brow. Norman Hague Hope was living at 14 Banks. Married to Charlotte Eliza Jackson in February 1908, they had both previously been living at 44 Far Banks. Whilst, in this case at least, this is known, it should be noted that the registers cause some confusion as addresses are variously referred to as Banks or Far Banks. Lottie Hope does not appear on the electoral register alongside her husband until 1919. That is presumably after the introduction of the Representation of the People Act 1918 that, after decades of campaigning by the Suffragists, finally allowed women over the age of 30 the right to vote.

Allowing some women the vote was just one of the outcomes from World War I. From 1914 to 1918 war dominated life in Britain and Honley did not escape the horror and loss of life. Honley Civic Society has published two books on the impact of the Great War on the village. *Honley in the Great War*[19] was published in 2014 to mark the centenary of the start of the conflict and *Honley Remembers*[23] was published to coincide with the 100th anniversary of Peace Day, held in July 1919 to welcome the soldiers home. Both books acknowledge the loss of almost 100 Honley lives.

A collective social conscience manifested itself in many ways from the outset of the conflict and the residents of Banks and Far Banks were no exception. At the start of the war, Margaret Sykes, the wife of Oswald Sykes at Far Bank, opened her home to provide a few beds for wounded servicemen. As the need for the facility grew, a new Auxiliary Hospital was built at Moorbottom next to the recently built Congregational Church. Margaret had a key role in the management of the new hospital and one of the first nurses engaged to care for the wounded was Nellie Holdroyd.

Honley in the Great War also makes reference to some other Banks and Far Banks residents. Harry Marsden, as the manager of the gas works, was involved in discussions about the supply of utilities. Keith Sykes, who lived at The Mount, was awarded the Military Cross for his work as a platoon leader and a newspaper cutting tells of the loss of Sgt Albert Victor Robinson, aged 21 years, whose family lived at Hillcrest.

It is unclear how the war impacted on Holdroyds, but a workforce of up to 30 had shrunk to just 16 by 1917. There may be others but records illustrate how one employee left to play his role in history. Willis Bray was born on 31st December, 1889 and started working for Holdroyds in May 1903 earning around 4s. 0d. a week. He disappears from the wages ledger in early December 1915, the date coinciding with his enlistment in the 21st Battalion West Yorkshire Regiment. He went to France in July 1916 but was killed in action on 27th March, 1918.[19]

In April 1916, Esther Heap died. Born in December 1838, she would have been 77 years of age. This is confirmed by the 1911 census, which shows her, then aged 72, to be still

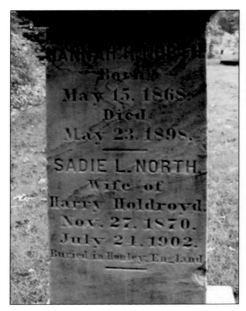

A Holdroyd family grave in Honley cemetery also bears the names of both Sarah and John North, making reference to their home town of Woonsocket. The separate graves (*above*) provide a link between places that are more than 3,000 miles apart.

Charley Holdroyd's name is beneath that of his daughter, Beatrice, who died aged 18 months. His name is followed by that of his wife, Emma Letitia and their daughter Ellen. With its gold lettering, it is, undoubtedly, one of the more elegant gravestones in the cemetery.

AFFECTIONATE REMEMBRANCE
OF
BEATRICE
THE BELOVED DAUGHTER OF
CHARLEY AND EMMA LETITIA HOLDROYD
BANKS HONLEY
BORN MARCH 12TH 1885
DIED SEPTEMBER 27TH 1886
Also of
CHARLEY HOLDROYD
BORN MARCH 26TH 1853
DIED MAY 8TH 1918
Also of
EMMA LETITIA HOLDROYD
BORN MAY 4TH 1854
DIED APRIL 14TH 1930
Also of
ELLEN BELOVED DAUGHTER OF
CHARLEY & EMMA LETITIA HOLDROYD
BORN APRIL 2ND 1879
DIED JANUARY 5TH 1962

running the Wheatsheaf Inn on Southgate. Her gravestone is in Honley Cemetery and records indicate that she would have died a wealthy lady. Probate was granted to her son, John Edward Heap, solicitor, her effects having been valued at £1,842 17s 2d.[1] These effects would have included the house at 14 Banks.

Two years later, in May 1918, Charley Holdroyd died. Born in March 1853, he was 64 years-of-age. Of all the Holdroyds, Charley seems to have been the most ambitious, acquiring property as it became available and building the business up to become a significant player in the Honley community. He was still on the electoral register for 1915 but, given that the country had more pressing matters to deal with, there are no records for the following two years for anyone.

Mary Jagger does not have a monopoly on seeing the poetry in history. The photograph (*opposite*) of Charley Holdroyd's grave in Honley Cemetery was taken on 8th May, 2018, the 100th anniversary of his death.

The Probate record indicates that, at death, Charley was worth £7,125 5s 1d, a substantial amount of money and, by 2018 calculations, a little under £3 million[11]. Sons Harry and Norman are identified as his executors. However, the record also shows that Charley died at Scalebor Park in Burley-in-Wharfedale, a hospital and, somewhat alarmingly, identifiable as one of several County Asylums run by the West Riding of Yorkshire. It is described as being akin to that at Storthes Hall, near Farnley Tyas, which was built in 1904, two years after Scalebor Park.[24] However, although such hospitals were built to house 'pauper lunatics', they are also known to have often supplemented their income by taking private, fee-paying patients. It is probable that Charley's last illness would not have been related to his mental health, but rather that his residence at Scalebor Park was an indication that he would have been able to afford the best nursing care for whatever ailed him.

Apparently, Charley Holdroyd liked to drink, which may ultimately have been his downfall. There are stories of him spending his evenings with his friends at Seth Senior and Sons' brewery in Shepley, after which he would be helped into his carriage to be returned home safely by his trusty horse. Such behaviour appears to have an impact on both his eldest son and his grandson who would spend their lives practising 'moderation in all things'.

After all his hard work in making the business a success and his accumulation of much wealth, failing health meant that Charley Holdroyd's empire was passed on to a new generation, that is to Harry. It is hoped, however, that he might have liked the idea of still being in the thoughts of at least one Honley resident 100 years after his death.

The probate record for Charley Holdroyd

HOLDROYD Charley of Banks Honley near **Huddersfield** died 8 May 1918 at Scalebor Park Burley-in-Wharfedale Yorkshire Probate **London** 25 March to Harry Holdroyd and Norman Holdroyd joiners.   Effects £7125 5s. 1d.

The marriage entry for William and Nora Beaumont.
High Street Wesleyan chapel Honley where the Beaumonts' marriage took place

In 1924, the year after the dissolution of the business between Herbert Scholefield and Norman Hope, Bradshaw Mills burnt down.

NOTICE is hereby given, that the Partnership heretofore subsisting between us, the undersigned, Herbert Scholefield and Norman Hague Hope, carrying on business as Woollen Manufacturers, at Bradshaw Mills, Honley, near Huddersfield, in the county of York, under the style or firm of "HERBERT SCHOLEFIELD & CO.," has been dissolved by effluxion of time as from the 27th day of January, 1923. All debts due and owing to or by the said late firm will be received or paid by Philip Wm. Chapman, of Bradshaw Mills, Honley.—As witness our hands this 29th day of January, 1923.

HERBERT SCHOLEFIELD.
NORMAN H. HOPE.

BANKS: 1918 TO 1933

Records from the wages ledger show that in January 1918, four months before Charley Holdroyd's death, his grandson introduced a fifth generation into the family business established by John Holdroyd in 1817. Harold North Holdroyd was 15 years of age when he started as an apprentice on a wage of six shillings a week. Rising quickly through the hierarchy, he would be at the helm for the next 55 years.

Within a short time Harold's responsibilities had increased, more so after Holdroyds diversified into the funeral director business. As coffin makers, they would doubtless have been involved in funerals for some years but May 1922 seems to mark a key development. This is the date from which a huge and impressive order book records the details of every funeral undertaken. Meticulous records give details of the deceased, together with the preferences of the family. Costs relate to coffin styles, the number of bearers, transport needs and all other related services. The costs vary widely according to requirements, but attention to detail is apparent in every record all the way through to November 1972.

Following Charley's death in 1918, his widow, Emma, had the properties at 4 and 6 Banks separated and number 6 was rented out to William and Nora Beaumont. William was born in 1875 and in the 1891 census is shown living with his family in Lower Hagg. At the time of his marriage to Nora, he lived in Upper Hagg. Nora Lodge, born in 1877, was from Park Gate, Berry Brow. He was a cloth finisher, she was a woollen weaver.

William and Nora married in July 1898 at the High Street Chapel in Honley and lived at Reins, Huddersfield Road, a short distance from Honley Bridge, before moving to 6 Banks in 1919. They would be there for the rest of their lives. When William died in March 1943, the record of his burial was certified by his neighbours, E Holdroyd & Co, in their role as funeral directors. Cross-referencing this with the entry in the order book gives all the details of his funeral. Nora remained at Banks until she died in March 1951, she and her husband both being buried in Honley cemetery. The probate record shows that she died at St Mary's Hospital, which was on the site of the former Deanhouse workhouse, Thongsbridge and that effects valued at just under £2,000 went to Harold Beaumont, co-operative society secretary and Ernest Jessop, a cloth designer.[1] Again, Holdroyds organised the funeral for their former neighbour.

In respect of number 14 Banks, by 1920, the Hopes had moved on to Imperial Road, Edgerton, Huddersfield. A manufacturer of woollen and worsted cloth, Norman Hague Hope had evidently been working for Herbert Scholefield & Co, a local woollen manufacturing business based at Bradshaw Mills in Honley. However, an item in The *London Gazette*, dated 2nd February, 1923 outlines the dissolution of his partnership with Herbert Scholefield. This parting of ways was due to 'effluxion of time', that is, the expiration of a time-limited agreement or contract.

New York 92	L'pool	Fallwood	Florence	..London..S..	DeMn	Teacher		45		England		1
	4	Footman	Beatrice	Salterford Rd, London S.W.17, Westwoods.		H'wife		26				1
	5	Gilbert	John	Hatchend, Middlesex, Clifton Hill House, Bristol.		Insurance Technologist	23	22		U.S.A.		
	6	Gilchrist	Grace	35, York Rd.								
	7	Guy	Charles	Canterbury, Streetley.		None	68			England		1
	8	Hobbs	Wilfred	Birks. Oxford. England.		Chartered Accountant	21					1
	9	Morris	Wm. R.	Boston Cottage,		Motor Mfgr.	48					1
	100	Holdroyd	Mary	Honley, Nr. Huddersfld.		H'wife		50				1
	1	do.	Harold	do.		Builder	23					1
	2	Hill	Maria	10, Kenwood Rd, Streatford, M'chester		Domestic		78				1

Harold and Mary Holdroyd on the RMS Carmania *passenger list from 1925*

In 1924, the year after this dissolution of the business, Bradshaw Mills burned down. From 1920, 14 Banks was occupied by its actual owner, Ronald Butterworth who had bought the house after Esther Heap's death. Ronald was born in 1890 and brought up at Broadfield, Holmbridge, Holmfirth. This large detached property, suggestive of considerable wealth, is now the site of Broadfield Park, a housing estate built in the late 1990s. Ronald's father was Frederick William Butterworth, born in 1864 in Hinchliffe Mill, who, in 1889, married Annie Louisa Woodhead. Annie was born in Netherthong in 1867. Her father, John Woodhead, was a woollen spinner who, in 1881, employed 'nineteen men and forty-five young people'.[26]

In 1911, aged 20, Ronald lived with his maternal uncle, 42-year-old Joseph Edward Woodhead, in Netherthong. Joseph had, by this time, taken over the running of the mill from his father and with no children of his own he may have taken on his sister's eldest son with a view to eventually passing on responsibility for the mill and the workforce. Ronald married Muriel Mary West in Blackburn in 1918, although she is not shown on the electoral register until 1924. Their children Joseph and Patricia were born in 1920 and 1924.

In 1924, the Butterworths moved to Hagg House in Netherthong before moving to Town Head in Honley in 1931, where Ronald remained for the rest of his life. Appearing to have always enjoyed financial security, the probate record shows that, when he died in December 1960, his effects were worth £9,500. He had still been living at Town Head, Honley, in an impressive property named Kirkside at the top of Church Street.[1]

Ronald Butterworth had rented out 14 Banks for several years before moving into it himself, but it was again destined to be a rental property when, on 22nd February, 1924, he sold the house and the adjacent land to Littlewoods Ltd. A record of this conveyance appears in a later document that summarises a number of historical transactions.

The document also makes reference to an 'Indenture of Conveyance', dated 8th April, 1924, between (1) Tom Allen Thornton and (2) Harry Holdroyd, in respect of an area of land of 1,330 square yards, property 'now or formerly' of George Fredrick Thornton. This purchase of the additional Ryecroft land further added to that owned by the Holdroyd family business. The Thorntons had been at Ryecroft at the time of sale of the first section of land by Joe Jessop but, by 1911, Tom Allen Thornton, a cloth dyer and finisher, lived with his wife at Fern Leigh. This house is directly behind Ryecroft and, being 14 Far End Lane, has often been confused with 14 Banks.

Soon after this event, Harold North Holdroyd made a trip to the United States. His return on the *RMS Carmania* in September 1925 is recorded and also shows that he went with his step-mother, Mary Annie Holdroyd. It also appears that Harry may have chosen not to accompany them. Aged 23, Harold was following in his father's footsteps and doubtless going to visit the family of a mother he had never known. He would maintain some contact with his American relatives throughout his life.

In her book, *I Remember ... My 1920s Childhood in Honley* Margaret Lumb (nee Kinder) writes about a trip to the theatre in Leeds. 'On one occasion a gentleman on the train gave me a whole shilling, the only time I remember such wealth all in one coin. He was Mr Holroyd, for whom my mother had been housekeeper before she met my father.' It is acknowledged that there must have been numerous Holdroyds in Honley but, whichever of the gentlemen this was, it's good to think of them as being so benevolent. They couldn't have known that such a small act of generosity would be remembered throughout Margaret Lumb's life.

When new, the properties at 40 to 46 Far Banks had been rented out, but within a few years, three of the five were occupied by members of the Holdroyd family, although they seemed keen not to actually live next door to each other! Norman and Amy were still at 48 and were joined in 1923 by Lewis, Evelyn and Charles Leslie who moved from Hagg Leys to number 44. Lastly, Harold North Holdroyd moved into number 40 with (Margaret) Winifred (nee Thornton) after their marriage in September 1929. Charles Leslie moved the short distance to Bradshaw Road in 1933, but his parents remained where they were until Lewis's death in 1951. Norman and Amy were there until 1956 and Harold and Winifred until 1955. The properties in between were occupied by the Marsdens until at least 1939 and by members of the Drake family from 1913 to 1987.

Following the sale in 1924, number 14 passed into the ownership of Littlewoods Ltd who were then in possession of it until 1931. France Littlewood is signatory to the document for the business which had its head office at Grove Mill at the bottom of Gynn Lane. The house must have been bought by Littlewoods to rent out again as electoral registers show it to have been the home of Ralph Moulton Bilton and his widowed mother, Marion Cooper Bilton, from 1924 until 1932. Ralph was born in Yeadon in 1895 and, at the time of the 1911 census, was a chemist's assistant there. His father, Thomas Arthur Bilton, a house painter, died in 1912 and Ralph and Marion moved to Shipley before coming to Honley in 1924. Ralph is listed in the 1927 *Kelly's Directory*, a trade directory and effectively the *Yellow Pages* of its time, the significance of the entry being that it is the first specific reference to 14 Banks being named as Banks House.[1]

In 1933, the Biltons moved the short distance from Banks to Oldfield Road before moving back to Wharfedale a few years later. However, they were still at Banks House when the next property transfer took place.

The conveyance dated 22nd January, 1931 was between (1) Littlewoods Ltd and (2) Harry Holdroyd of Boston Cottage, Banks and Harold North Holdroyd of Far Banks. Littlewoods were referred to as the estate owner; Edward Holdroyd and Sons were the purchasers. The sale price was £625 on what the document refers to as a 'partnership property'. As a consequence, Holdroyds now owned all of Banks from the boundary with Netherfield to the start of Upper Banks. This included all the buildings associated with the business as well as all the residential properties at 2 to 14 Banks and 16 and probably 38 Far Banks.

Harold North Holdroyd as a young man

Following demolition of John Holdroyd's original workshop, a new building was constructed to house the expanding funeral services business

In 1928, the old workshop building between the offices and Boston Cottage was demolished. This would have been the site of the original joinery business where John Holdroyd established the enterprise that his son would eventually put his name to. It can be seen on the 1854 map, is recorded on the 1871 census and appears in the 1905 pictures. By 1930, Holdroyds had constructed a new building that would eventually become the offices and garage for the funeral business that had evolved from their work in cabinet and coffin making. It is apparent from the photograph above that the columns on number 10 were not added until after these new premises had been built. When added, they introduced style to the house.

It might have been assumed that their construction had been inspired by properties that Harry had seen whilst visiting New England in the United States. Unfortunately, and somewhat disappointingly, local knowledge reports that Harold Holdroyd later asserted that his father had had the columns added, not for their aesthetic impact, but rather to stop people tripping over the front doorstep that protrudes onto the pavement! Maybe the truth is somewhere between the two versions of events.

When Emma Letitia Holdroyd died in April 1930, her daughter Nellie continued to live at number 4. Her brother Harry and his wife Mary were still at number 10, Boston Cottage, numbers 2 and 8 were still occupied by the Jillotts and William and Nora Beaumont were still at number 6.

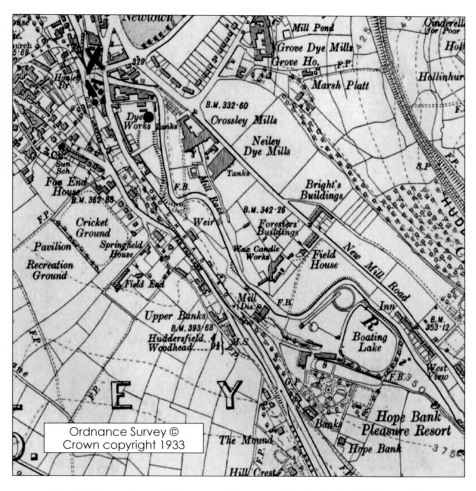

The 1933 map shows the terrace of houses at Far Banks, just to the south-east of Upper Banks. The Hope Bank Pleasure Ground, at this time enjoying considerable popularity and success, is also shown.

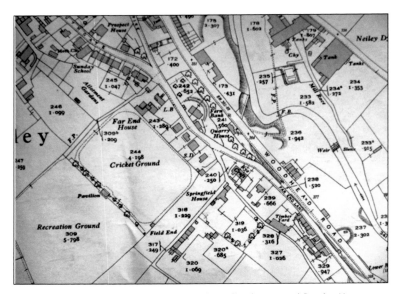

The 1932 Ordnance Survey maps show the houses at Banks, Upper Banks and Far Banks in even greater detail. On this, the timber yard at Banks is identified. Other landmarks shown are: Quarry House, Ryecroft, Lower Banks Mills (disused), the Methodist Church on Southgate, the 'switchback railway of the pleasure ground and a candle factory across the river that was, somewhat ironically, destroyed by fire in 1976.

Ordnance Survey © Crown copyright 1932

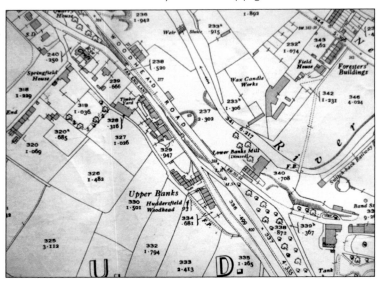

BANKS: 1933 TO 1940
AND THE 1939 REGISTER

With Holdroyds now the owners of 14 Banks, the property was again rented out for a number of years. In 1933 and 1934, it was occupied by Frederick William Taylor and Hilda Beatrice Taylor. Then, after two years with no record of anyone living in it, it became the home of the Dickinson family. The house may not actually have been empty, it may just be that the occupants were not entered onto the electoral registers for those years. Such gaps in available information, although frustrating, are inevitable. They also ensure that there is always more to learn.

The amount of information about places, people, their families and their work had steadily increased from the minimal detail of the 1841 census, through to the much more helpful 1911 one. Electoral registers provide additional information and even the production of telephone directories can serve to confirm property occupation details.

In more recent times we take the amount of information available for granted and improvements in technology have increasingly allowed vast amounts to be collected and stored. It may be noted that concern about how information relating to individuals and virtually every aspect of their lives is used, has become a modern day problem, so much so that yet more legislation has been required to control its use. However, future seekers of records will find a frustrating lack of data between the censuses of 1921 and 1951.

In these days of multiple data back-ups, it is astonishing to learn that when the 1931 census records were destroyed by fire during World War II, they were the only copies! All the work that had gone into collecting so much valuable information ... for nothing! More understandable, is the absence of a 1941 census as one was not taken due to the ongoing conflict and the national need to be sparing with information that could be used by the enemy. However, with war declared, a record was made of the population in 1939 as part of the necessary preparations.

The 1939 Register was taken on 29th September, the information then being used to produce identity cards and ration books. It was also used to administer conscription and to monitor the movement of a population that was subject to military mobilisations and mass evacuations. The relatively recent inclusion of the register on genealogy websites has been a very welcome development.

In the electoral register for 1937, the occupants of 14 Banks were shown to be Walter, Fannie, Kathleen and Roy Dickinson. By 1939, they had been joined by Doris (nee Hutchinson) who married Roy in 1938. The 1939 Register also records that Walter Dickinson was a 58-year-old machine designer. His skills were evidently to be used in the military as he is noted to be an airman in the R.A.F. The occupation of Fanny is listed, as with most of the other women of the time as 'unpaid domestic duties'. Daughter Kathleen was a 34-year-old clerical worker, listed as covering Clerical A.R.P Control, a reference to the work of the Air

```
HOUSING INSPECTION,HOUSING ACT, 1930..

Report on Nos. 18, 20, 22, 24, 26, 28, 30, 32, 34,
        and 36, Far Banks,

Owned by the trustees of Mr. Walter Middleton
deceased,(or Mrs. Mary Roberts c/o Messrs.Heap,
Marshall, & Heeley, Station Road, Holmfirth.

(John Turner of Station Road,Holmfirth,Agent)
```

	No. 18, Far Banks.	(Mrs.Butterworth)
Living Room.	Stone flags, worn and uneven.	
	Windows, Scullery window defective,other windows insufficient light.	
	Fireplace, Defective, out of date.	
Bedroom.	Floor defective, (usual decay)	
Pantry.	No Pantry, food kept in Scullery.	
Closet Accommodation.	(Privy Midden) Insufficient and inefficient.	
Ashpit Accommodation.	do. do. do.	
Roof.	(Grey slates) require overhauling.	
Eaves gutters.	Defective, require overhauling and painting.	
Down Spouts.	Defective, do. do.	
External Walls.	Require pointing on front.	
Approach to houses.	Path leading to houses, open space in front of houses, and back road leading to houses needs repairing.	

The first page of the 1934 Housing Report into properties at Upper Banks

Raid Precautions Service. Her brother Roy, aged 29, was an engineer, whilst his wife, Doris, was a 24-year-old shorthand typist.

There are, understandably, no electoral registers for the years 1940 to 1944 and in 1945, only Walter and Fannie are shown at the address. By 1946 Kathleen had returned to her parents' home, where they were also joined by Frances Dietrichstein. Walter died in July 1946 and, in 1947, only Fannie and Kathleen were shown. Then, from 1948 to 1951, just Fannie and Frances Dickinson were living at number 14. The name change suggests that Frances may have been a relative of Walter's who came to England to join a family that had, like many others before them, assumed a change of name after World War I to counter anti-German feeling. The similarity in the names Dietrichstein and Dickinson make this suggestion probable. Walter's probate record identifies him as 'Dickinson Walter of Banks House Banks Honley Huddersfield'. Effects valued at £109 went to his son Roy.

The 1939 Register lists all the other residents of Banks. It tells us that 81-year-old Kate Jessop and her domestic servant Lily Sharp were still at 1 Ryecroft. Norman and Nellie Waite were at number 3. Norman was a ruling-machine maker (in the family business of Waite and Sheard), an air raid warden and a representative of the West Riding County Council. Number 5 was occupied by Harold and Ada Thornton. Harold was a master cloth dyer and finisher. Next door, at Netherfield, were George and Lily Thornton, who had been there since the house was built sometime around 1929. He is shown to be a retired master dyer. Thomas Jillott, dyer's labourer, and his wife Sarah were still at number 2 Banks, sharing their home with Kathleen Newies, a 19-year-old shorthand typist for a chemical works. Nellie Holdroyd was still at number 4 and William and Nora Beaumont at 6. His occupation was given as woollen and fine worsted cloth finisher. He may have worked alongside his neighbour, Emily Jillott, a woollen and fine worsted cloth mender, who was still living with her sister Hannah at number 8.

Harry and Mary Holdroyd were still at number 10 in 1939, his occupation given as that of a joiner and builder (partially retired). He was also recorded as being a volunteer with the A.R.P. service. The properties between the Holdroyds and the Dickinsons are not shown, being redacted and marked 'This record is officially closed'. Was the existence of a joinery business deemed politically sensitive? Actually, such redaction is common within the register, which tries to avoid listing people who may still be alive or where insufficient information exists for the record to be safely released to public view.

Cecil Hobson who, with wife Martha (known as Patti) was at 16 Far Banks from 1930 to 1951, was also a joiner and assigned to the ARP Rescue and Demolition unit of the Home Guard. He was joined in this unit by Harold North Holdroyd who, as a funeral director and coffin maker, was also designated ARP for Civilian Deaths. Beyond Harold and Winifred at 40 Far Banks, were Florence Drake and her daughter, Maggie, a building society clerk. Number 44 was still home to Lewis Holdroyd, a wood machinist, and wife Evelyn. Gas works manager, Harry Marsden and his wife Laura were still at 46. Electrical engineer, Norman Holdroyd and his wife Amy shared their Sunny Bank home with Alice Young. Alice appears alongside them in most records providing at least 20 years of domestic support. This may be accounted for in part by the 1939 record which notes Amy, who was always seen to be in poor health, to be incapacitated.

At Norwood, Frank Robinson, a drapery store manager, was living with wife Annie and son, Douglas, who worked alongside him. Also in the retail business was Fred Moss who, with wife Clara, was at Glen Dene. He was the general manager of a Co-operative store. Charles Thornton, at Wood View, a retired cloth dyer and finisher, was also noted to be with the Special Constabulary.

A particularly significant change to the Banks landscape which began in the late 1930s was the apparent and somewhat abrupt disappearance of Upper Banks. The properties were still marked on the 1950 map, but electoral register records for 18 to 38 Far Banks stopped in 1938. The 1939 register marked number 18 as a 'closed record' and all the properties from 20 to 36 Banks with the letter 'V' only, presumably a sign that they were now vacant.

After many years of possible inattention from the landlords, the properties had fallen into a very poor state and a housing report in 1934 carried out under the 1930 Housing Act on numbers 18 to 36 Far Banks effectively condemned them all. The properties are noted to

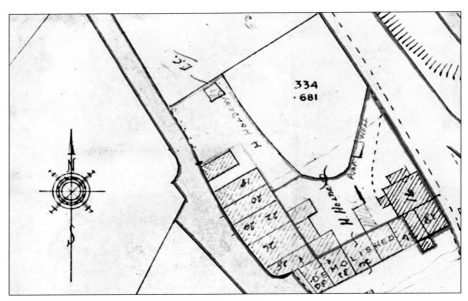

The plan *above* is undated but shows the individual properties at Upper Banks. The houses along the bottom, 32 to 36, are noted to have already been demolished. These exclude numbers 16 and 38 which are nearest the road and which, along with much of the land, were then owned by Harold North Holdroyd. A footpath to the rear of these two properties passes the pump and well, which had been the only source of water. Properties are of different sizes, although they all adjoin one another, numbers 22 and 24 appear to be the only ones which are back-to-back.

be owned by the trustees of Mr Walter Middleton (deceased) or Mrs Mary Roberts, c/o Messers Heap, Marshall & Heeley, Station Road, Holmfirth. Each report identifies the current occupant and then lists the defects of the property. They all highlight similar issues - uneven floors, defective windows, no pantry and roofs, gutters and downspouts that needed attention. With no sewerage in place, the houses also relied on a privy or ashpit midden which was, by way of understatement, noted to be 'insufficient and inefficient'. By the time we reach the report on number 32 it's hard not to view the need for a new front door to be a little superfluous.

Over the next three years, all the occupants from 20 to 36 moved out. Electoral registers show that a number of them relocated to the new houses that had just been built on Long Lane. Emma Butterworth, Harry Brook, Alex Coldwell, Norman Hirst and Frances Boothroyd were the last to go. All are to be commended for their fortitude in remaining for so long.

In earlier times Upper Banks must have been a close community. From electoral register and census records it is clear that families lived there for many years. Brays, Smiths, Boothroyds, Brooks, Schofields and Wilsons were all there for several decades. Other than names on records, we know little of the lives of any individuals, although Fred Graham who was at number 28 from 1903 to 1911 is understood to have managed the horses for Holdroyds and Tom Smith, who was a local gamekeeper, was at number 28 and then 26 from 1887 until 1919.

The housing report doesn't mention 38 or 16 Far Banks, so they may have been in good repair. The latter evidently remained for much longer, Fred and Lillian Battye were the last occupants, leaving in 1962. This may have accounted for 16 Banks being given a house name when it was built. In addition to their purchase of Banks House and its adjacent land from Littlewoods, the map indicates that Holdroyds had bought all the remaining land between Banks and Far Banks. Maybe this was on the understanding that they would oversee or assist with the demolition of the old houses. They now jointly owned all of the land and all the properties from the boundary with Netherfield right through to 40 Far Banks.

Fred Graham outside Banks House in the 1920s, with two of his charges

Gamekeeper Tom Smith, who doesn't look like someone you would wish to meet if you were up to no good in Hagg Wood!

BANKS: 1940 TO 1965

Harry Holdroyd was born in November 1874 and died in January 1951 aged 76 years. Perhaps the most adventurous of the Holdroyds, he was remarkably well travelled. In addition to his visits to the United States in the 1890s, he continued to enjoy regular trips around the world in his later years with his wife Mary Annie. Apart from these travels, Harry lived his entire life at 4 and then 10 Banks. In addition to his working life being spent in the service of Edward Holdroyd and Sons, he was a very active member of the wider Honley community.

Charley Holdroyd had been a member of the Honley Urban District Council from 1894 to 1904 and Harry from 1904 to 1936 retiring only when the council merged with that of Holmfirth. For most of this period Harry was the chairman, being re-elected a number of times due to his popularity. In a vignette in the *Huddersfield Examiner* dated 15th January, 1938, he was referred to as the 'Father' of the Council and his commitment and works were enthusiastically acknowledged. He was involved in many local institutions including those connected to the school and church and his attendance at over 3,000 meetings and his role on many committees placed him at the heart of many local decisions. In respect of his work as a builder, the article states that 'he took a prominent part in preparing the plans for the new houses which were built on Honley Moor and these are now recognised as some of the best built by any council in the country'.[27]

In addition to their other properties, in 1938 Harry and Harold North Holdroyd had bought Bleak House in the centre of Honley, together with the garden across the road from it. At the end of 1950, discussions were taking place about the best use for an amenity that was so central to the village and these were still ongoing when Harry died. A local press report notes that his last wish was that 'the park might become public property'. Although it has had some less attractive times in the years since, the Honley Old People's Park has recently benefitted from investment and attention and is still a community asset for the people of Honley. It was central to the Honley Remembers events in July 2019 (*page 95*).

Probate records show that, in 1951, Harry Holdroyd and his brother Lewis died within a few months of each other. There appears to be a marked difference in their worth, which suggests the value placed on the joinery business and its associated property portfolio. The online comparison suggests that £20,148 could be worth as much as £2,694,000 at today's prices.[11] Probate was granted to Harry's widow, Mary Annie and to his children, Harold North and Marion Beatrice. Four years later, in May 1955, Mary died. Her property, valued at £7,061 was left to 'Harold North Holdroyd, joiner and builder and Beatrice Armitage, a married woman'.

After Harry's death Mary had shared her home with Clara Sykes, who was a housekeeper and companion. Clara then remained at the house to support Norman Holdroyd who moved to Boston Cottage from Far Banks in 1956 after his wife moved into a care home. He

FOR nearly a hundred years there has been a Holdroyd prominent in the public and business life of Honley. The present representative of the family, Councillor Harry Holdroyd, of Boston Cottage, Honley, has been connected with almost every public body in the village and many others outside.

No matter what kind of work there has been to do or how long it would take to do it, Councillor Holdroyd has volunteered and carried it out to the best of his ability.

The Father of Honley Council, from The Week's Vignette, cuttings from *Huddersfield Examiner* of 15th January, 1938.

Probate records of Harry Holdroyd and his brother Lewis.

HOLDROYD Harry of Boston Cottage Banks Honley **Huddersfield** died 16 January 1951 Probate **Wakefield** 27 April to Mary Annie Holdroyd widow Harold North Holdroyd joiner and builder and Marion Beatrice Armitage (wife of Norman Armitage). Effects £20148 10s. 3d.

HOLDROYD Lewis of 44 Far Banks Honley **Huddersfield** died 29 June 1951 at St. Marys Hospital Deanhouse Holmfirth Yorkshire Probate **London** 22 September to Charles Leslie Holdroyd electrical engineer and Evelyn Irene Holdroyd widow. Effects £215 12s. 9d.

Bleak House and garden in Westgate. The summer house is on the left.

remained there until his death in October 1959. Despite her apparent frailty, Amy survived him by 18 months. In 1957, Norman's great nephew, Kenneth Holdroyd, moved there with his wife, Elizabeth.

It is poignant to read the entries in the funerals order book when it comes to close family members. They are recorded in detail as are all the others, but it is clear that no expense was spared for the occasions. Harry's funeral is the first in the book to cost more than £100, albeit by just sixpence. This is significantly more than the average family paid. Even more was spent when it came to Mary's funeral. The records deal in practicalities and finance, but there is also a sensitivity that comes across in many of them, especially where child burials are concerned. The costs are always much lower, with one recording the almost token charge of £2 15s to enable grieving parents to bury a baby that had been stillborn.

Many of the residents of Banks and Far Banks disappear from the story only to return via a final appearance in the funeral book. Sometimes the information provided ties up some loose ends. When Joseph Hall died in October 1939 aged 65, he and his wife Daisy had been living a short distance away from Honley in Berry Brow. Daisy died in 1951, aged 70. The Hopes evidently remained at Imperial Road, Edgerton for the rest of their lives. Norman died in August 1951 aged 71 years. Charlotte died in January 1960 aged 81 years. William and Nora Beaumont, Joseph and Daisy Hall, Norman and Charlotte Hope, Ronald Butterworth, Walter Dickinson, Hannah, Emily and Thomas Jillott, and even Mary Ann Jagger herself, all join numerous other neighbours and family members within the pages.

With Harry's death, the family business was now in the hands of Harold North Holdroyd. In 1953, registration as a company meant a change in name to Edward Holdroyd and Sons Ltd. The distinctive dark red wooden signs from the outside of the premises that are still in existence probably date from this time.

Sometime during the early 1950s, Harold North Holdroyd had the former access road to Upper Banks alongside number 40 filled in, probably using materials from the derelict houses. He then used this space to create a garden which comprised a large grassed area with very high walls down to the house and road and up to the now empty land above. In November 1955 he and Winifred, together with now grown up sons, Malcolm James and Edward Julian, moved into Turnstones. This house had been built in the space immediately beyond 48 Far Banks and was therefore now number 50. Photos show it to have had an extensive garden which included an arboretum and a large allotment area. The house at 40 Far Banks was then occupied by Harold's recently widowed mother-in-law, Margaret Thornton, until her death in 1964.

From 1952 to 1959, the electoral registers show 14 Banks to have been occupied by William and Mary Lockwood and their two children. Prior to moving to Banks, the Lockwoods had lived, albeit briefly, at Bleak House in the centre of Honley that was, or had been, owned for a time by the Holdroyds. The families were well known to each other and the children of both had played in the large garden opposite, next to the old police station, before it was gifted to the village. The garden included a summer house and Julian Holdroyd recalls sheltering in this from torrential rain one spring day before returning home to Far Banks and noting with the excitement of a small child that the River Holme had burst its banks and filled the valley below. The Whit Monday flood of May 1944 is recorded as one of the more significant events in the history of the Holme Valley.

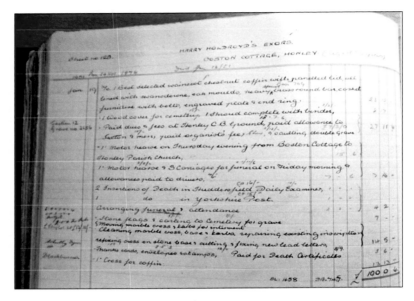

The record showing the details of Harry Holdroyd's funeral

'Plan referred to' this time in use when the land attached to Banks House was sold

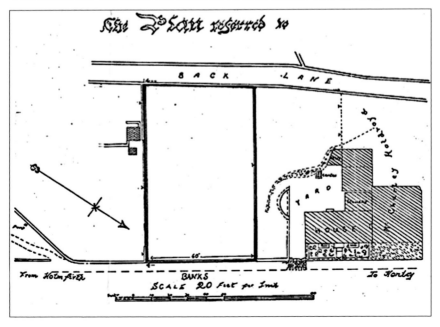

There is a Deed of Appointment dated 7th April, 1959 in which Harold North Holdroyd of Turnstones, Far Banks and Nellie Holdroyd of 4 Banks are identified as trustees. It is by now apparent that clarification of trustees usually precedes another property transfer. This took place on 15th April, 1959 and relates to a conveyance for the sale of the land adjacent to Banks House that had until this point been linked to the property. The sale was of the 'land with a 60 foot frontage of Banks', by Harold North Holdroyd and Nellie Holdroyd to Arthur Lupton Littlewood, of Woodlands, Station Road, Honley, a worsted cloth exporter, and Freda Littlewood. The price paid for this area of land was £150. The dwelling house, Banks House and its associated buildings, were to be 'retained by the vendors'. A condition of the sale was that the purchasers could sell the land for development or build a house, but they could not run a business from it, nor could they keep livestock!

The same 'plan referred to' is used as in 1903, although the road name has been updated. Also, the land south of the area for sale is no longer marked as being owned by Mary Roberts. Despite his death in 1918, Charley Holdroyd's name still appears on the map as the owner of the land occupied by Edward Holdroyd and Sons Ltd. A complete copy of this plan is at Appendix 3.

This land with the 60 foot frontage was used to build the bungalow, named Cotswold, the property now numbered 16 Banks. The land beyond, which also belonged to the Holdroyds, must have been sold at the same time as two other bungalows, numbers 18 (Sheraton) and 20, appear to have been part of the same building project. To accommodate these, the last properties at Upper Banks were also demolished. On the back of the photograph of the 1910 Renault on page 54, a note states that, when 16 and 38 Far Banks were demolished, the stone was then used to build 20 Banks for the Robinsons. Only the ground floor of number 16 was kept to be converted into a garage. All three bungalows were built to their new owners specifications by Holdroyds. The Littlewoods had evidently had the house built for their own use as they were living at this address from 1960 to 1972.

The electoral registers currently recorded on the Ancestry website end in 1961. From this point information about the occupancy of the houses at Banks and Far Banks had to be obtained from the records kept in the Local History section of Huddersfield Library. In the interests of confidentiality, people are only identified by name if they no longer live at Banks.

Ellen (Nellie) Holdroyd died in January 1962. Nellie was born in April 1879, so would have been aged 83 years. She was buried with her parents, Charley and Emma Letitia and is named on their gravestone. She never married or had children, but pictures suggest a huge affection for, and a lifelong interest in, the nephew who had lost his own mother. It is likely that she played a significant role in Harold North's life in his first few years, particularly those years before Harry remarried. Nellie worked for some time as a nurse, most notably at the Auxiliary Hospital during the Great War and is remembered very fondly by those who knew her.

For the last 11 years of her life, Nellie shared her home with Jane Mellors, a companion and perhaps carer. The probate record identifies Nellie as a spinster. It also notes that effects valued at £3,020 18s 5d went to Harold North Holdroyd, master builder.[1] Apart from a known visit to the United States in 1902, Nellie had lived her entire life at number 4 Banks.

From 1960 to 1964, Wilbert and Nellie Dewes (nee Perkin) were living at 14 Banks, along with Nellie's mother, Beatrice Ellis, then almost 80 years old. Wilbert was born in Leeds in March 1921 and in 1939 was a chartered accountant living with his widowed father and a sister at Argyle Street. Nellie was born in May 1918, also in Leeds, living at Hartwell Terrace with her mother and a sister. In 1939, all three women were in the tailoring business, with Nellie also working for the British Red Cross. As with a number of records for women on the 1939 register, the name Perkin has been crossed out, and been corrected to Dewes to acknowledge Nellie's marriage to Wilbert in Leeds in early 1942. The couple ended their days in Bury, Lancashire, dying within a month of each other in spring 2000.

The Dewes left the area in 1964 and the regional phone directory then shows Kenneth Irwin Holdroyd to be living at Banks House. Kenneth, the son of Charles Leslie and Elizabeth Irwin, and therefore Lewis Holdroyd's grandson and Charley Holdroyd's great-grandson, had moved there from his family's home at Boston Cottage. By 1968, he had moved to Moorside, Long Lane. Born in February 1935, he died in 2003.

Nellie Holdroyd

BANKS: 1965 TO 1975

S oon after we moved to Honley, a doorstep salesman arrived offering an aerial photograph of Banks. It isn't a very good photograph and we might not have been interested had it not been for the date the picture had been taken. On the reverse, we are informed that it was taken on 28th June, 1966.

The picture (*page 80*) shows the Holdroyds joinery and construction business still active, along with the timber yard. The only element missing is the original chimney that stood somewhere behind the shed to the rear of the offices. At the top left of the picture is one of the three new bungalows, Cotswold. Just below is Banks House, 14 Banks, adjoining the offices and workshops of Edward Holdroyd and Sons Ltd. The garage seen in an earlier picture has been replaced with the 1930 building which had become the premises for Holdroyds Funeral Directors. To the right of this is Boston Cottage, 10 Banks, the columns just about visible, followed by the cottages at numbers 8, 6, 4 and 2. Back Lane runs along the top of the wood yard and the main Woodhead Road is below a wooded slope.

Across the years, the fortunes of Holdroyds seem to have come from its ability to successfully evolve to meet changing times and new demands. The original joinery had expanded into house building and other construction work. This later included electrical engineering, not something that would have troubled the newly created business of 1817. Early joinery work to create furniture and cabinets would have also included coffin making leading to the development of the funeral business. Early assumptions that the large upstairs bay window on the 1930 building had served some loading purpose for the joinery proved incorrect. It was actually installed to maximise light in the offices. Similarly, the idea that the garage on the ground floor was for funeral cars was not the case. These were actually provided by the garage run by Kilner and Brooke, half a mile away at Newtown. In *Honley Bridge and Newtown* we learn that when the partnership ended,

> *Charlie Brooke continued the garage, taxi and charabanc hire business supplying wedding and funeral cars. The latter were in conjunction with E Holdroyd and Sons of Far Banks, joiners and undertakers.* [14]

Kenneth Holdroyd's move from Boston Cottage into Banks House in 1964 indicates the start of a process of significant change for Banks. However, number 10 was not sold at this time. From 1965 to 1976, it was occupied by Wilfred and Olwen Greenwood. Wilfred was the manager for the Holdroyds businesses at Banks, so renting the house would have enabled him to remain close to the site throughout what was probably a challenging time.

Kenneth Holdroyd rented Banks House until 1968, when he was followed by Paul and Margaret Brothwell. We were once told by the people who we bought the house from that it had been rented out to a local curate at some point. That Paul Brothwell was a curate at Honley Parish Church meant another question answered. He and his wife Margaret, who was the daughter of the Bishop of Lichfield and a nurse, only lived in it for two years. The

An aerial photograph of Edward Holdroyd & Sons Ltd, in 1966

The premises of Edward Holdroyd & Sons Ltd, in 1972, with the maroon sign clearly visible alongside the large window, with (inset) two of the Edward Holdroyd & Sons Ltd signs

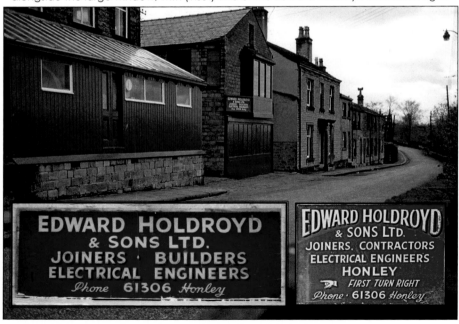

electoral registers then show no-one in occupation from 1970 to 1975; it seems that the empty house was used by Holdroyds primarily as a storage facility during this time.

The social landscape of the 1970s was very different to that of even 20 years earlier. A rise in consumerism would not have included craftsmen-built furniture. National unrest, seen in strikes, power cuts and a three-day week, would probably not have been an immediate issue for Holdroyds, but they would have had an impact on their workforce and on their wider business opportunities. Also, technology was beginning to advance at an alarming pace and young men were no longer expected to follow their fathers into a family business. Change was inevitable and as the 1970s got underway, events began to mark the beginning of the end of the joinery and wood yard business.

A document that records the various sales of property actually begins with a memorandum relating to a conveyance dated 21st December, 1965 in which a property was to be sold by Harold North Holdroyd to Walter Gerard Pollitt. It had initially been assumed that this was number 10, coinciding as it does with Kenneth Holdroyd's move from the house, but evidence from electoral registers indicates that Walter and Mildred Pollitt moved into number 40 Far Banks in 1967 following the death of Margaret Thornton, Harold's mother-in-law, three years earlier.

A further record, dated 1st April, 1970, notes the sale of the plot of land that is the wooded slope between Banks and the Woodhead Road as well as the woodland immediately across the A6024. This agreement was between (1) Harold and his son, Edward Julian Holdroyd and (2) Edward Wrigley Aubrook, John Newton Broadbent, Marcus Alan Ellis and Gordon Ripley who were all Trustees of the Huddersfield Naturalist Antiquarian and Photographic Society. This information initially appeared to address the long-standing question as to who the land actually belonged to, however, the organisation appears to have ceased existence or been subsumed into another in the intervening years. Furthermore, the larger part of the land, that is the three acres between the road and the river, appear to have been sold on to The Woodland Trust in 1988. It isn't clear if this transaction included the wooded slope in front of Banks.

On 14th June, 1973 an application was made for an official land search as part of the process of identifying a replacement Trustee following the death in 1962 of Nellie Holdroyd. On 19th June, 1973, (Edward) Julian Holdroyd, also of Turnstones, Far Banks was identified as taking this role on alongside his father. Julian's occupation was given as that of a chartered accountant indicating that he had chosen to follow a different career, specifically that of his maternal grandfather, James Mallinson Thornton. Maybe Harold North Holdroyd had felt some pressure to follow his father into the family business, but he seems to have encouraged his children to make their own career decisions. In 1983 Julian married Tessa Ransom in Sussex. Tessa came back to Yorkshire with Julian and went on to make a name for herself for her considerable support of her new community. Her interest in politics led to her standing as a possible election candidate for the Colne Valley constituency in 1987. The *Huddersfield Examiner* carried an obituary to her after her death in March 2016, which noted that she had been tireless in her voluntary work and that she had been awarded the OBE in 1996.[28]

Julian's older brother, James Malcolm Holdroyd, also appears to have preferred to use his middle name as those who remember him refer to him as Malcolm. Like his brother, he had also elected not to join the family business, choosing to study law, before deciding on a career in the church instead. Following his death in November 2010, the *Yorkshire Post* carried an obituary which noted that 'he was the elder of two boys, their father Harold running the family joinery, building and undertaking business – Edward Holdroyd and Sons Ltd – which had been going since 1817'.[29] The obituary notes that Malcolm Holdroyd was ordained as a priest in 1961. He was a curate in Brighouse before becoming a vicar in Barnsley and then in Marsden. He then moved south to Brighton, where he remained for 19 years until he retired in 1993. He then returned to live with his parents at Turnstones.

20th June, 1973 is the date of a conveyance between (1) Harold North Holdroyd & Julian Edward Holdroyd and (2) William Mallinson & Sons (Lockwood) Ltd, based at 205/207 Lockwood Road, Lockwood. The schedule referred to 'all that piece of land situate at Banks, Honley, together with the dwelling house known as Banks House'. This comprised all of the property except the plot of land with the 60 foot frontage, which had been sold to the Littlewoods in 1959 and the cottages at numbers 2 to 10. It is a very significant event, as it represents the wholesale selling off of the business of Edward Holdroyd & Sons Ltd, as well as the dwelling house at number 14. It is this conveyance document that provided the initial information about some of the additional historic transactions:

- *The 1888 transfer of land – 1,351 sq yds – between Joe Jessop and the Holdroyds*
- *The 1897 agreement between Joseph Green and others, and Charley Holdroyd relating to the cottages*
- *The 1903 sale of the joiners shop, garage and connected buildings by Emma Hoyle and Walter Middleton to the Holdroyds*
- *The 1924 transfer of land – 1,330 sq yds – between the Thorntons and the Holdroyds*
- *The 1931 sale of 1,275 sq yds of land including the dwelling house to the Holdroyds noting the subsequent 1959 sale of the land with 60' frontage to the Littlewoods.*

The Trustees agreed to the sale of all of their Banks property, including the dwelling house known as Banks House to William Mallinson and Sons (Lockwood) Ltd. The funeral business was taken over by Highfield Funeral Directors, based in Huddersfield.

In 1973, Harold North Holdroyd would have been 71 years of age, past retirement age, and disinclined to press either of his sons into taking over the family business. With an initial payment of £5,000 made by William Mallinson, the remaining £15,000 was loaned to him by Harold, who essentially sold the property under a private repayment agreement similar to a mortgage. The terms of the financial element of this schedule make up the larger part of the 1973 document. Although the repayment term was to be five years, later information indicates that the loan was paid in full by December 1975.

Documentation dated 20th November, 1973 notes that, following their expansion, Wm Mallinson & Sons (Lockwood) Ltd, changed its name to Wm Mallinson & Sons (Yorkshire) Ltd. Archive information shows them to have been builders and quarry owners. Perhaps they intended to incorporate the timber yard and business into their own enterprise but, after only two years, they were already preparing to sell their Banks holdings.

BANKS: 1975 TO 1986

Just to catch up with some of the other Banks residents. In September 1970, ten years after moving to the newly built 16 Banks, Arthur Littlewood died, aged 85. The following year his widow Freda sold 'Cotswold' to John Herbert Lee and his wife Annie (nee Wilson). They moved there with their daughter Margaret Brenda Lee (known as Brenda). John had at one time been a schools attendance officer and the bungalow was evidently their choice of home to spend their years of retirement. John Lee died in June 1981 aged 84 and his wife Annie died two years later aged 81. Brenda remained in the house, later sharing it with a great nephew whose upbringing she took responsibility for. Brenda was a head teacher and, during the 1970s, had been appointed as the President of the Huddersfield and District Head Teachers Association. She was the first woman to hold this post and used her acceptance speech to comment on the recent introduction of the Sex Discrimination Act and to call for more female heads of junior and secondary schools. Following her retirement, she opened and ran a nursery school for a time. Always active, in 1984 she was the chairman of Thongsbridge Tennis Club and was a very keen golfer. She lived at Banks until her death in April 2015 at the age of 79. We had then been neighbours for almost 30 years.

Number 18 Banks, Sheraton, had been bought from new by Arnold and Alice Tinker. Alice died in September 1976, but Arnold remained there until 1980. In 1983 it was home to Barrie and Anne Mallinson. Maybe the Mallinsons were related to the company that bought Banks in 1973, but it's more interesting to wonder if the Tinkers were descendants of a family who had been at 34 Upper Banks in the 1910s. Number 20, the third of the bungalows was home to George and Irene Robinson from 1964. They left in 1975 and John and Margaret Hawkes moved in, staying until 1978.

At Far Banks, the Pollitts remained at number 40 until 1988 when they sold the house to Nicholas and Catherine Flynn. Maggie Drake, whose family had been in number 42 since 1913, was there herself from 1930 to 1987. Harry and Gladys Smith, who were at 44 from 1954, sold to Rodney and Jean Elgie in the mid 1970s and the Fishers who had moved into 46 in 1953 had gone by 1993. The Quantrills were at number 48, Sunny Bank, from 1958 to 1965, when they sold the house to John and Gladys Babbings. All the houses have since changed hands again at least once.

The date of 18th August, 1975 is recorded for a land search which was carried out ahead of Banks House being sold again. On 20th February, 1976 a land charges act certificate notes: 'Protection ends on 12 March 1976'. The history of the property and its composition of numerous elements means that, with ever increasing rules and regulations, its sale may have been a particularly complex process. A requisitions on title document, relating specifically to Banks House and dated 4th February, 1976, suggests some petulance on the part of legal advisers who were seeking clarification on a number of possible issues.

•   *A request for Title Documents is responded to as follows: 'No documents will be delivered on completion save the Conveyance to the Purchaser since we are retaining a right of way we will keep the title deeds'.*

•   *To the request, 'Please forward to us evidence of passing of title from Esther Heap to Littlewoods Ltd.' The response is, 'Is this not before the root of the title?'*

•   *To the request, 'Please forward an abstract of the title of Harry Holdroyd'. The response is, 'Do you not have an Abstract of the Conveyance 22nd Jan 1931?'*

•   *To the request, 'Please forward an abstract of the title of Nellie Holdroyd'. The response is, 'Nellie Holdroyd was only a Trustee who was replaced by the Appointment dated 19 June 1973'*

The first point indicates that the property was to be sold, but that Mallinsons would retain the original right of way via the driveway and rear of the house to the other properties still in their possession. A further complication may have been that, by the time of the actual sale, Mallinsons had already sold the adjoining properties that is, the wood yard, the warehouses, workshops and offices, complete with the access via the rear of Banks House, to other buyers. One of these was Jack Brook, a local builder.

By 12th April, 1976, the complications appeared to have been sorted out and William Mallinson & Sons (Yorkshire) Ltd sold Banks House to William and Jacqueline Butterworth for £8,950. An impressive parchment document has been signed and sealed to this effect. Prior to finalising the house purchase, Jacqueline Butterworth negotiated directly with Brook for the purchase of some additional land that had been part of the access right of way. This then allowed for the removal of said access, ensuring greater privacy and some additional garden space at the rear of the kitchen. It also enabled the building of a low wall topped with fencing to separate the property from the adjacent building, the former workshops of Edward Holdroyd & Sons Ltd. The purchase of the additional land added a further £1,000 to the price of the property, but doubtless removing the right of way issue was worth the cost. This agreement was between the Butterworths and Jacqueline Brook.

Eighteen months later, the cottages were also sold. A memorandum dated 20th October, 1977 notes that number 6 was sold by Harold Holdroyd to Gladys Grindall. Prior to this, the house had been home to Cecil and Martha (Patti) Hobson who had occupied it for 25 years since relocating from their former home. From 1930 to 1951 the Hobsons had lived at the last surviving dwelling at Upper Banks, Hamer Bray's old house at number 16.

On 25th October, 1977, numbers 2 and 4 Banks were sold to David and Janet Stringer. Number 2 had been empty since Sarah Jillott had left in 1976 and number 4 had had an uncharacteristically unstable few years since the death of Nellie Holdroyd in 1962. The house, which had been home to the Holdroyd family for at least 160 years, had seen a number of occupants during the previous 15. From 1964 to 1966, it was rented by Cyril and Anne Haigh and for some of that time also by Barbara and Bryan Mannock. These people may have had a connection to Holdroyds. Certainly Cyril Haigh was employed for a time as the bookkeeper. Charles and Edna Barker were there in 1967 and 1968 after which there are two years with no record of occupancy. In 1972 it was taken over by Elsie Whiteley and her daughter Jean, but only Elsie was there in 1977.

During the same period, number 10, Boston Cottage was sold to John (Sean) and Eileen Kenny and, finally, on 15th December, 1977, number 8 was sold to Ada Berry. Emily Jillott had been there until 1963, ending over a century of Bray/Jillott tenancy. For the 12 years prior to her purchase of it, Ada Berry had been renting the cottage. After she left in December 1985 it was bought as a rental property by Maureen Emsley, Janet Stringer's mother, who had worked for Harold North Holdroyd in the capacity of wages clerk and administrator.

Harold North Holdroyd having sold all the dwellings and Mallinsons having sold the other properties on the site, the whole area then underwent a significant redevelopment. The land where the timber had been stored and which had originally been bought from Joe Jessop and Tom Thornton, was sold to Reginald Brian Senior, a field sales engineer who, in the early 1980s, built a large and impressive bungalow initially named Westwood View. He lived in this house, using the remaining land to build a further two similar bungalows, Jordene and Arncliffe. All three properties have gardens and wide driveways to the front. Westwood, as it now is, also has an access road at the rear, running parallel to Back Lane. These three properties occupy the land between the houses at Banks and Netherfield.

The remainder of the Holdroyds' buildings having been sold by Mallinsons to Jack Brook's building company, the large sheds at the rear of the cottages were demolished, leaving the ground floor structures intact as potential garage or workshop space. The factory offices and workshop building and the 1929 building that had housed the offices and garage of the funeral business between this and Boston Cottage, would both later be converted into houses.

By the end of 1977, Edward Holdroyd & Sons Ltd, Joiners, Cabinet Makers, Contractors, Builders and in its later years, Electrical Engineers and Funeral Directors officially established in 1817, no longer existed. The Holdroyds had been in business at Banks for over 160 years.

Banks in 2005

Banks in 2018

BANKS: 1986 TO THE PRESENT

The book *Then & Now Honley*, by Peter Bray and Honley Civic Society, presents the picture on page 86 alongside an earlier one with the Holdroyd workforce outside the premises. This one may have been taken in around 2005, 100 years after the first.[17]

The columns can be more clearly seen on Boston Cottage, in the photographs on page 86. Number 12 occupies the place where the original joinery once stood, the large upstairs window showing where the office of the funeral directors was. The markings above the large window and front door on 12a are the only evidence of the frontage of the former workshops. The corner of the garden at number 14, Banks House, is just visible.

Bill and Jackie Butterworth lived at Banks House for ten years during which time they had two children. They also travelled extensively and for at least one period of two years, possibly more, they were in the Middle East. Metal bars had been custom-made to protect the rear windows during these absences and the somewhat forbidding old gates had been retained as added security. Foreign travel was a regular feature of Bill's work and he had to make a swift return from Dubai at the end of 1986 to attend to the paperwork required ahead of the next property transfer.

On 4th December, 1986 contracts were exchanged on the sale of Banks House by William and Jacqueline Butterworth to us. We moved in, along with our 18-month-old son, a week later.

Following some confusion about the additional land purchased in 1976, the solicitor came to view the property soon after we moved in to double check the accuracy of the plans contained in the house deeds. It was discovered that the agreement between the Butterworths and the Brooks in respect of the purchase had never been linked to the Land Registry records. A new document, dated 19th January, 1987 now officially confirmed the earlier transfer of land thereby removing any future confusion. By coincidence, the solicitors who oversaw the conveyance processes for us were Messrs Heap, Marshall and Healy of Holmfirth, the same company who had assisted in the purchase of Banks House by Esther Heap from the Middleton family in 1903. This historic connection may account for some of the old records being included in the package of papers that came back to us in 2008.

Five months before we moved in, in July 1986, the dwelling house newly converted from the offices and workshops was sold. This then became 'The Banks', 12a Banks. The house created from the former offices of the funeral business at number 12 was initially named Hope Bank House, but this may have been dropped as the original house with that name was still where the pleasure ground used to be. Number 12 last changed hands in 1998. Boston Cottage, 10 Banks, last changed owners in January 2008 when the Kennys, who had been there from the 1970s, moved a short distance away. David and Janet Stringer at number 4 still also owned and rented out the cottages at numbers 2 and 8, until they moved to Upper

Hagg in 2004 and into another Holdroyd built house. Numbers 4, 6 and 8 Banks all changed hands again as recently as 2015.

Although not actually part of Banks, Quarry House still exists. During the late 1980s, it was a restaurant called The Captain's Table. Some years later it was sold and after refurbishment was resurrected as Mannions. This project was fairly short-lived and it has since been converted back to a dwelling house.

For as long as I can remember my father always had a painting on the go. Photography was both his profession and his hobby but anything artistic seemed to be within his skill set. I loved how he could transform an old black and white picture into something that was colourful and vibrant, our walls always held holiday pictures that had been brought to life in this way. When we moved to Honley in 1986, our interest in the history of the village even then led us to the photograph of the tram at Honley Bridge dated 1907. Dad's more usual subject for paintings was steam trains, but he made an exception and presented us with a painting of the scene, shown on the back cover of this book. I later learned that trams were also special to him as his own grandfather had been a tram car conductor, when London United Tramways began electric traction in 1901 in the Clapham area of London. Our interest in the history of the area prompted Dad to change the advert on the front of the tram to read, 'Holdroyd Builders Honley'. The painting is now on display at Honley Library.

During the 1990s, our boys spent some years with a child-minder, Katy Flynn, who lived at 40 Far Banks. Together with Nick and Katy's two boys, they used to play on the empty expanse of land at the side of the house which Harold North Holdroyd had levelled to create a play area for his boys. Unknown to us then, this was where some of the original houses on Upper Banks had been. When developers moved onto the site in 2002 to build a new house, they apparently discovered that the earlier properties had had cellars, necessitating a vast amount of hard core to fill in the ground to ensure its stability. With a choice of any number from 22 to 38, and the option to select Far Banks or Banks, the owners of the new house elected an address of 36 Far Banks.

The discovery of the existence of the houses at Upper Banks has been especially satisfying. The intriguing gaps in numbering and the change from Banks to Far Banks has long been something of a mystery. Whilst we guessed that 'something' must have occupied the space, the disappearance of Upper Banks was complete, so finding this lost community has been very rewarding. No-one is around now who remembers them as being lived in, but those 12 houses at Upper Banks were people's homes, the places where the Bray children would have played with the Smiths, Schofields, Holdroyds and Middletons. By modern standards their amenities were seriously lacking, but there is a sense of community within that small block of cottages on the old maps. Sadly, the photographs provide very limited information, but the stone garage in front of number 20, being at road level, may be the only remaining piece of physical evidence of the buildings and community that existed above it. However, if the old stone from some of the houses was indeed used in the construction of number 20 Banks for the Robinsons, perhaps Upper Banks is still with us in spirit.

In 1961, as the large gardens of old were gradually being given up, a new house was built in the grounds to the rear of The Mount; this is The Bungalow. In more recent years another property has been built at road level, this is now numbered 62a. Around the turn of the century, yet another new house was built between Far Banks and Turnstones, sited on the area that was originally the Turnstones vegetable garden. This, The Bungalow and other houses now extend Far Banks to land behind Woodview, Norwood and Glen Dene. In the early 2000s, around the same time that the new house was being built where Upper Banks had been, another development was underway a few yards along Far Banks. This was on the site where the large property Hillcrest had been. Only built around 1919, it was demolished in the 1980s and the site cleared. This was also used to build a new house, by far the largest in the area. To their credit the new owners retained the original name.

We never did get to meet Harold North Holdroyd, but Julian believes that his father would be pleased that knowledge of his family business lives on and there are still a number of people around who remember him with admiration. Since finding reports of his many talks to various organisations on local history, I believe that he would approve of this book. Like his father, Harold North was an active member of the Honley community. He was a manager of the Honley CE(C) Junior School for 45 years. A member of the Honley Good Companions, Chairman of the National Federation of Funeral Directors (Huddersfield) and President of the Holmfirth Rotary Club. If they are a reliable measure, his numerous scrapbooks of newspaper cuttings illustrate a very wide range of interests.

Before his belated retirement, he had been the fifth generation Holdroyd to run the family business. He was born, in the saddest of circumstances, in July 1902, never knowing his birth mother, 'American Sarah'. This was the year before Esther Heap bought Banks House at auction for £354, and three years after the Victoria Tower on Castle Hill – Huddersfield's most iconic landmark, which is visible from Banks – was opened to commemorate Queen Victoria's Diamond Jubilee.

Harold North Holdroyd, builder, joiner, electrical engineer and funeral director, the last of the Holdroyds on Banks, died in August 2001. He was 99-years-old.

Harold North Holdroyd celebrating his 90th birthday in 1992.

HOLDROYD GRAVES

An original photograph of one of the Holdroyd graves in Honley Cemetery
which marks the resting place of Sarah Louise Holdroyd (nee North) The
picture on page 91 shows the group of gravestones with the original cross
elevated and tablets for other members of the Holdroyd family
A view of the entrance to Honley graveyard

HOLDROYD GRAVES - INSCRIPTIONS

IN LOVING MEMORY OF
SARAH LOUISE (SADIE)
WIFE OF HARRY HOLDROYD
AND DAUGHTER OF JOHN NORTH
OF WOONSOCKET R.I. U.S.A.
BORN 27TH NOVEMBER 1870 DIED 24TH JULY 1902
THY WILL BE DONE
ALSO THE ABOVE NAMED JOHN NORTH
WHO DIED AT HONLEY 24TH AUG 1914
IN HIS 70TH YEAR
ALSO THE ABOVE NAMED
HARRY HOLDROYD
BORN NOVEMBER 24TH 1874 DIED JANUARY 16TH 1951
ALSO MARY ANNIE
WIFE OF THE ABOVE NAMED HARRY HOLDROYD
BORN FEBRUARY 7TH 1875 DIED MAY 11TH 1955
ALSO
MARGARET WINIFRED
DEAR WIFE OF HAROLD N HOLDROYD
BORN 7TH JUNE 1906
DIED 8TH AUGUST 1997
AND
HAROLD NORTH HOLDROYD
SON OF HARRY AND SADIE
BORN 18TH JULY 1902
DIED 31ST AUGUST 2001

POSTSCRIPT

Banks House being our third house in six years, I could never have envisaged us still being here more than three decades later. If we estimate its earliest possible occupation to be around the mid 1850s, when the Middleton family first took up residence, it is apparent that we have now been here longer than any of the previous occupants. It had been empty for five years before the Butterworths moved in and we know that they were away from it for long periods of time. By 1986 both the house and garden appeared to us to be in need of some care.

As previous owners did, we have made many changes to it, particularly in the early years. We had a new window put into the living room and another into the large bedroom ahead of dividing the room into two. This followed the arrival of our second son in 1989. It seemed appropriate to enable the boys to each have their own room; a very different situation to the days when the Holdroyds lived here with at least ten of their children.

In October 1993, a somewhat insubstantial 'lean-to' that had provided a rear lobby and workroom was demolished and replaced with a larger stone-built extension. The builder sought out old stone to ensure a match with the existing house and managed to acquire this from the recently demolished Kings Mill on Kings Mill Lane in Huddersfield. We also sold a wood burning stove and replaced it with a gas fire after the former brought us worryingly close to a conflagration. We later also replaced an open fire with an electric one, accepting the limitations of 'artificial flames' as a trade off for cleanliness and ease of use.

We replaced all the old windows in 2001, finally losing the broken and draughty old sashes with the 'rolled glass' panes that gave looking through them a sense of drunkenness. When we upgraded the kitchen in late 2006, we had a second window installed to overlook the patio. The accommodation of a new cooker meant extensive work to the chimney to meet modern building regulations. This area would have been where 14-year-old Emma Lindley, or later on Lucy Burks, might have used a range to prepare meals for the Middleton and Hall families. We then refurbished the bathroom the following year, watching with a mixture of horror and relief as the plumber took a sledgehammer to the century-old pot bath. In 2007 we had extensive work to the roof to cure some fairly long standing leaks.

Only once has the house actually let us down. On the evening of 24th December, 1997 gale force winds caught the gable end and brought the original, huge and very heavy, chimney pots down. Their fall to earth was broken by the roof of our Ford Fiesta parked in the driveway. The story has often been told of what Santa did to our chimney on that particular Christmas Eve!

To bring us up to date, in October 2012, we had solar panels fitted to the roof; we can only wonder what Edward, Edwin, Charley or Harry Holdroyd might have made of that particular development! Of course, these were just the major house improvements; other significant changes having also taken place throughout our time here.

Naturally, we've had our grumbles about the activities of those who were here before us! Who thought it was a good idea to tack sheets of hardboard to all the panelled doors? And whoever imagined that a dark green tiled fireplace would look good beyond the 1940s? And why was the landing window, the only one that looks out onto the garden, totally opaque?

Of course, future occupants may look at our own contributions and sigh with exasperation, 'what were they thinking of?'

On the outside, the house has looked very different. For many years it was covered in ivy which reached to the guttering on both the front and side. We had planted it to try to soften the plain stone, not expecting it to grow so prolifically. Eventually, keeping it in check proved too difficult. It came down in stages but the house still looks somewhat bare in comparison to past times!

The garden presented an even bigger challenge than the house, the larger part of it being situated on top of the bank, the Meal Hill referred to in old documents. This means that the bungalow at number 16 sits in an elevated position some way above us, prompting the inevitable jokes about our neighbours looking down on us.

The hill, or bank, means that we, and our neighbours from 12a back to 2, have a rock face a short distance from the back door. A priority on moving in was to put a fence along the top to ensure the safety of an active toddler. Throughout the late 1980s we and our neighbours all rose to the challenge and managed to make gardens from the land 'up top'. This required access, for which we acquired an old industrial staircase enabling a direct connection up and over the shed and onto the garden. Neighbours also created access routes although – for some time – those at 12a used a long ladder tied, somewhat precariously, to a tree stump! For us, in addition to landscaping the top garden we also had to address the area to the side of the driveway. This also had to be completely landscaped, but into a steep rockery with steps and a path up through it as a second access route to the garden above. After the extension was built in 1993 we then paved the additional area of land, purchased by the Butterworths in 1976, to create a proper patio. In the summer this is a real sun-trap.

An original brick-built building, just across the road from the driveway and set down on the wooded slope, just out of sight, was the last remaining evidence of the Holdroyd business. An old photograph shows this to have originally been a two storey construction, probably used for storage purposes. In 2009 cracks appeared in the foundations, threatening to collapse the building onto the main A6024. In April 2010, the council finally agreed that it was unsafe and demolished it, closing the access gaps in the wall at the same time. Of course, such work prompted questions about the ownership of the land. There were rumours that Harold North Holdroyd had sold the land to a local amateur photographic group but, until now, we had never officially known this. The local council occasionally gives some attention to the trees if they start to hinder the buses passing below us, but not as much as they need. They did, however, carry out some work on them in 2014, ahead of the Tour de France cycle race. Whether anyone is still around to make a claim on the land is doubtful, but any claim should come with a warning. The local council might be interested in speaking to them about payment for works carried out!

And so, thirty plus years have somehow passed. When we first moved from Hyde in Greater Manchester in 1983, we lived in Scholes above Holmfirth. Our neighbours there pointed out very quickly that we would never be true Yorkshire people, but would always remain 'Comers-in'. Unlike Mary Jagger, I am not 'indigenous to Honley soil', but that doesn't stop me from having great affection for the village. Surely, once someone has lived in a place for more than half of their life, they should be allowed to adopt it as their own? Still, at least our sons can both claim to be Yorkshire men!

As noted earlier, I completed some family history research some years ago, covering a similar period of time. Should they ever be interested, our sons will have details of everyone from their own generation back to 30 out of 32 of their great-great-great grandparents. Only the Johannings are missing. Like the Dietrichstein / Dickinsons may have done, they came to this country from Germany in the 1850s and later changed the family name to Johnson to avoid any repercussions from a population that, at the time, had little inclination towards being friendly with those from a perceived enemy state. The change of family name only became apparent in 1985 when Granddad Johnson died and his birth certificate was found. The disinclination of past generations to share personal information is a frequent hindrance to present day researchers, but maybe some mystery is better than the modern need to share everything with everyone!

Many, many people have been identified within the family's history, half of them with the genes that I carry. From Middlesex to South Shields, East Anglia to Manchester, many via Leicester and the East Midlands; numerous individual lives are captured in records for posterity. I know their names, relationships and occupations. I have seen who employed servants and who were the servants, where fortunes have been made and where tragedy has struck. But they are spread across a geographically wide area, and few of the ancestors have resonated with me quite like the people who walked the stone slab pavement in front of our house, who looked out from our windows and admired the same views across the Holme Valley and who ate and slept under our roof and who lived and worked on Banks.

Our move to Honley in 1986 was undoubtedly a very successful one. The area is very attractive and visitors are always very complimentary about it. Of the people we have known who have moved away, few have ever moved more than a very short distance! Our boys went to the local schools and now both have homes of their own within a few miles of us. Banks House was a very worthwhile investment in so many ways.

Of all the properties on Banks, number 14 is the one that has had the greatest number of residents. Middletons, Holdroyds, Gledhills, Halls, Hopes, Butterworths, Biltons, Taylors, Dickinsons, Lockwoods, Dewes. Then Holdroyds again. There are a few other long-term residents of Banks, most notably the Brays, the Jillotts, the Boothroyds and the Beaumonts. However, the history of Banks is primarily the history of the Holdroyds. Despite the efforts of Charley, and the good works of Harry and Harold North, their family profile remains surprisingly low in the village. There are no roads, folds or buildings named after them; even the donation of the Old Peoples' Park somehow slipped under the radar. They provided good quality furniture along with a number of other necessary services, but mostly they just got on with their lives. In *St Mary's Church and Honley – A Chronological Canter*, Bob Etherington summarised the life of the village and its people in 1888.

> *If a dyer, you might have been employed by Thomas Farrar; a miner, by Joseph Haigh, the Hall Ing colliery owner; a carpenter, by Edward Holdroyd, who no doubt would have buried you if Dr Smailes had not been able to cure you.*[7]

The occupation of any house can only ever be temporary; we are custodians of it for only a part of its history. One day, we too will need to leave, perhaps when we can no longer manage the steep double step into the cellar, or navigate the climb up to the top garden. Maybe this history will be of interest to the people still to come, who will then take their turn to occupy the house and make it a home.

In viewing Banks as a place, we can understand a little about its likely contribution to the life of Honley village as a whole. Having now discovered its existence, it is tempting to miss the little community at Upper Banks but, even in the 1930s, it would not have been practical to try to bring it up to modern standards. There now seems to be a good balance between the old and the new. In times of sometimes swift redevelopment, many of the old buildings have remained relatively unchanged for a century and a half. The houses aren't especially pretty - we don't go in for rose-strewn thatched cottages in this part of the country. The average Yorkshire person is far too grounded in practicality for that. As the observer looks along the row of plain stone cottages they will note that none of the exterior walls are straight and there is limited uniformity between each house, but they are all solidly built and will, almost certainly, be here for many years to come.

As for 'Banks' as a collection of people, we can only ever speculate on what took place within the walls of the houses, offices and workshop buildings. As I have been writing this, I sometimes sense people in the shadows, encouraging me to find out more. The quote from 'The Storyteller' on the front page relates to the work of the genealogist but, even though the people in this story are not related to me, it still feels relevant. Inevitably, there is some element of 'cold gathering of facts' in the necessary identification of dates and other details, but I hope that I have indeed been able to breathe life into Banks and its people.

'Those who have gone before cry out to us, "Tell our story!" So we do'.

Honley Old People's Park, formerly the garden of Bleak House, was central to the Honley Remembers events in July 2019

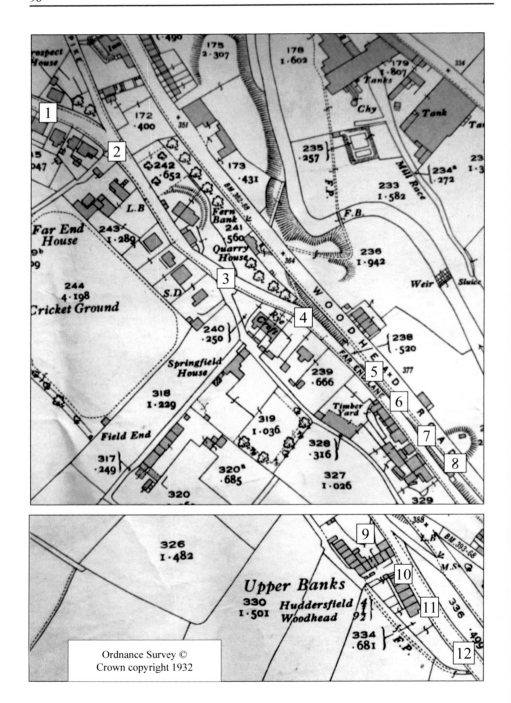

Ordnance Survey ©
Crown copyright 1932

APPENDIX 1: A WALK AROUND BANKS

S hould you feel inclined, you can find Banks a short walk from the centre of Honley. The walk is only short but a circular route may include a field path and the back lane. In poor weather parts of it may be muddy, so please be prepared for this. The maps are dated from 1932 so show the buildings and landscape as it was then. Upper Banks still exists, but all the properties built since then are missing.

From the centre of Honley village, follow Southgate. It is very narrow as it squeezes between the buildings. The house at the left side of the entrance to the newly built Southgate Fold was originally The Wheatsheaf Inn. Mary Jagger lived as a child in the post office that was part of the row of cottages that follow. There are several interesting properties along this part of Southgate, each with its own history to be researched.

Using the map opposite, the reference numbers correspond to the steps below.

1. On the right is the site of the old Primitive Methodist Church. This is now the car park for the Southgate Theatre that is housed in the old Sunday School building. The red brick house a few metres along on the right is where Mary Jagger was living when she wrote her *History of Honley* in 1914.

2. At the top of the Old Turnpike, Southgate reverts to its original name, Far End Lane. Pass the road up to the Honley Cricket Club and continue to follow the road away from Honley Village. On the right is Far End House, where Banks Mill owner William Haigh lived. The newer houses within the courtyard were created in the late 1980s from the outbuildings.

3. After a short distance Far End Lane forks off to the right becoming Field End Lane. Keep left so that you follow the road. There is no sign, but you are now on Banks.

4. The three houses at Ryecroft are above, followed by Netherfield. Note the footpath on the left that goes down to the Woodhead Road and Quarry House. The three newer dwellings set back from the road were built around 1978 – 1980 on the site of the Holdroyds' timber yard.

5. The houses that follow are the original 'Banks' buildings, the oldest probably dating from the early 1800s when the Woodhead Road was created as part of the original Huddersfield to Woodhead Turnpike route. Prior to this Far End Lane had been the main road from Honley to Holmfirth.

The cottages were probably part of the Banks Mill estate, the mill being in the valley below it. Much of Banks was later developed into the timber and construction business founded in 1817 by Edward Holdroyd. The only identification of Banks is the name plate on the first cottage. This is number 2. For many years it was home to members of the Jillott family.

6. Number 4 is a double property and was the home of the Holdroyds from at least the early 1800s until the 1960s. Number 6 was integrated into number 4 when Charley Holdroyd and his family were there. It was separated in 1919 and became the home of the Beaumonts. Number 8 was also occupied by the Bray/Jillott family from at least 1861 to 1963.

7. 'Boston Cottage' at number 10 – the house with the columns, was built by Holdroyds in 1900 for Charley's son Harry and his first wife. Harry married Sarah Louise in America so

the house was clearly named for a place was special to them both. The date and carvings of Kitchener can be seen around the door, but the columns were added several years later.

8. Number 12 was built around 1929 on the site of the original joiner's workshop; it has a large window on the first floor and was the offices of Holdroyds funeral services. 12a is named as The Banks as it was originally the offices and workshops for Holdroyds. It was built around the 1880s to adjoin the dwelling house, Banks House at number 14. Banks House had been built in the mid 1850s. All the houses from 2 to 14 have a rock face along the back, so gardens are at roof level. This can be seen most clearly at Banks House.

9. The following three bungalows are on the higher level and were built by Holdroyds in 1959/60. Two of these were built on the site of the original community of 12 houses that formed Upper Banks and which were demolished in the late 1940s/early 1950s.

10. A new house now bridges the gap that was previously a garden for number 40 Far Banks and, prior to that, the access road to Upper Banks.

11. This is followed by the five terraced houses, 40 to 48, that were built from around 1905 and which mark the beginning of Far Banks. Only the last one has a name, Sunny Bank.

In the valley below, an industrial park now sits where the Hope Bank Pleasure Ground once attracted visitors in their thousands.

> For a longer walk, you may wish to follow the road as far as the junction with Oldfield Road. This will take you past Turnstones and the older properties Woodview, Far Bank and The Mount. Despite the road climbing upwards, the houses become even higher. Imagine being the postman!

> At the crossroads, turn sharp right and take the road towards Oldfield. After a short distance turn right into Long Lane. When the road bends to the left take the footpath to your right; this is accessed by a stile and takes you down the edge of a field. The path will bring you out behind Hillcrest and back down onto Far Banks.

12. Retrace your steps to Turnstones. Between it and Sunny Bank, a gap in the wall hides some steep (and slippery!) steps leading to the footpath that eventually becomes the lane passing the back of all the houses on Banks. This will return you to Field End Lane and its junction with Far End Lane and the road back to the village centre.

OS MAP OF SOUTH-EAST HONLEY

The OS map dated 1892 (opposite) show the creations of the offices and other buildings at Banks as well as the establishment of the timber yard. The individual properties at Banks and at Upper Banks are clearer.

Ordnance Survey © Crown copyright

APPENDIX 2: MAP 1892

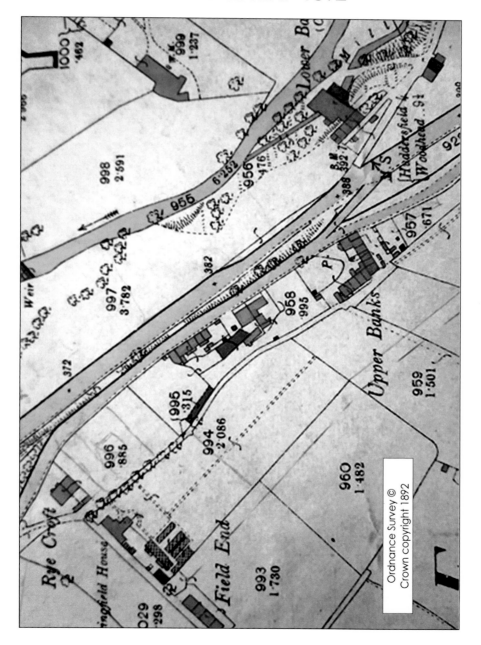

APPENDIX 3: PLAN OF BANKS, c1902

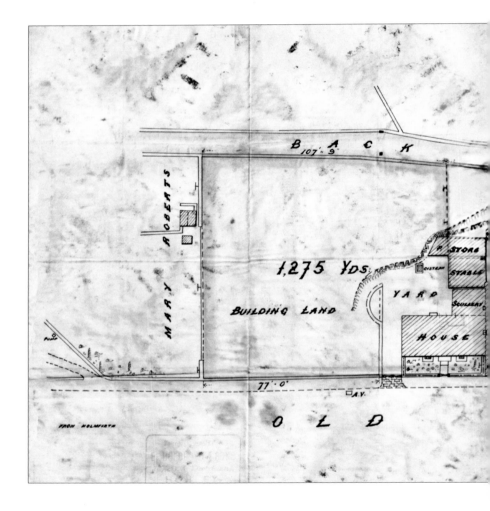

These two pages contain a plan of Banks, It must date from around 1902 as it is that used in the 1903 sale of Banks House. Charley Holdroyd has already bought the land from Joe Jessop, The road is still Old Turnpike and Boston Cottage has been built and named.

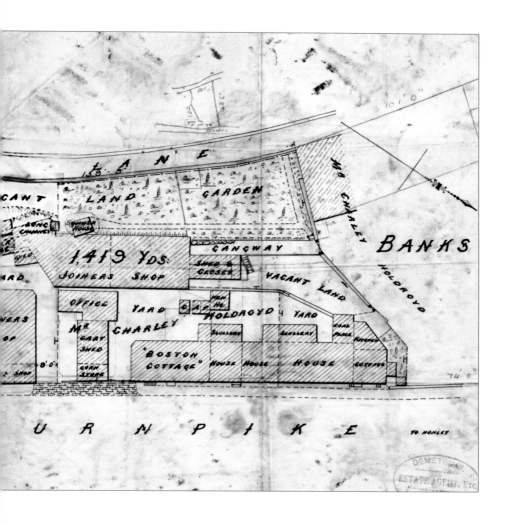

REFERENCES

W here appropriate, images that are in the National Archives have been included in accordance with the Open Government Licence for public sector information. A copy of the licence can be found at: http://www.nationalarchives.gov.uk/doc/open-government-licence/version/3/
All internet links were live at the time of publication.

1. Ancestry website: http://ancestry.co.uk
2. Huddersfield Exposed: a collection of articles and pages about the history of Huddersfield and the surrounding area https://huddersfield.exposed/wiki/Welcome accessed March 2018
3. Jagger, Mary. 1914. The History of Honley and its Hamlets from the Earliest Time to the Present Available in Honley Library and at: https://huddersfield.exposed/wiki/The_History_of_Honley_and_its_Hamlets_from_the_Earliest_Time_to_the_Present_(1914)_by_Mary_A._Jagger accessed March 2018
4. Streetmap.co.uk: http://streetmap.co.uk/loc/Honley – http://streetmap.co.uk/map.srf?x=413500&y=411500&z=120&sv=Honley&st=3&tl=Map+of+Honley,+Kirklees+[City/Town/Village]&mapp=map.srf accessed March 2018
5. Huddersfield Exposed: The Huddersfield and Woodhead Turnpike Road; https://huddersfield.exposed/wiki/Huddersfield_and_Woodhead_Turnpike_Road accessed March 2018
6. Masson, Ray 2013.Hope Bank – Honley's Pleasure Grounds and Gardens 3rd edition. Honley Civic Society
7. Etherington, Bob. 2004. St Mary's Church and Honley, a Chronological Canter. Honley Civic Society
8. Honley Town Book – 1746 to 1846. Transcribed and Presented by Shirley Manning Heaton. Souvenir Facsimile published by Honley Parish Church for its Quincentenary in 2003. The Enterprise Group, Honley
9. Day, Michael. 2013 Wool and Worsit – a History of Textiles in the Holme Valley, Laverock Publishing
10. Brooke, Alan, A Catalogue of the Textile Mills and Factories of the Huddersfield Area C.1790-1914. https://undergroundhistories.wordpress.com/a-catalogue-of-the-textile-mills-and-factories-of-the-huddersfield-area-c-1790-1914/ accessed March 2018
11. Measuring Worth. Website: https://www.measuringworth.com/calculators/ppoweruk/
12. The London Gazette, 26th July, 1892, https://www.thegazette.co.uk/London/issue/26310/page/4267/data.pdf accessed March 2018.
13. Ordnance Survey 1932 Map of Honley and Brockholes. Ordnance Survey © Crown copyright 1932

14. Marshall, Peter. 2013. Honley Bridge and Newtown. Honley Civic Society

15. Hamilton, Ed, My Old Ohio Home: S.M.North of Woonsocket, Rhode Island website: https://myoldohiohome.com/articles/s-m-north-of-woonsocket-rhode-island. php accessed March 2018.

16. Etherington, Bob, (based on research by) 2016 Honley National School 1816 – 1952. Honley Civic Society

17. Bray, Peter & Honley Civic Society 2006. Then and Now Honley. Tempus

18. Marshall, Peter. 2014. Honley Through Old Advertising. Honley Civic Society

19. Ford, Cyril and Honley Civic Society. 2014. Honley in the Great War 1914 - 1918' Honley Civic Society

20. Page, Caroline. 2015. Farnley Tyas a History. Honley Civic Society

21. Find A Grave, database and images https://www.findagrave.com/ memorial/48336980/sadie-l-holdroyd:, memorial page for Sadie L North Holdroyd, Find A Grave Memorial no. 48336980, Oak Hill Cemetery, Woonsocket, Providence County, Rhode Island, USA. Website maintained by Kevin Avery; accessed July 2018

22. Berry, Peter 2017 By Industry We Prosper The Holme Valley Lodge No.652: Its foundation and the history of the first one hundred and sixty years. http://hvl652.org/wp-content/uploads/2017/12/Lodge-history.pdf accessed June 2018

23. Marshall, Peter 2019. Honley Remembers – Village Life in the Great War. Honley Civic Society

24. Information on Scalebor Park, http://www.countyasylums.co.uk/scalebor-park-burley-in-wharfedale/ accessed March 2018.

25. The London Gazette, 2nd February, 1923. https://www.thegazette.co.uk/London/ issue/32792/page/858/data.pdf   accessed March 2018

26. Peter Sandford, White Rose Genealogy. http://www.familiesrevealed.com/Red%20 memo%20Book%20-%20Web%20publication%20v1-1.pdf accessed 16/04/2018

27. The Huddersfield Examiner 'The Week's Vignette: Enjoyed every minute of Public Work. The "Father" of Honley Council", dated 15th January, 1938

28. The Huddersfield Examiner, 14th March, 2016. https://www.examiner.co.uk/news/ west-yorkshire-news/obituary-tireless-volunteer-tessa-holdroyd-11035294   accessed April 2018

29. The Yorkshire Post, 19th November, 2010. https://www.yorkshirepost.co.uk/news/ obituaries/james-holdroyd-1-3025895 accessed April 2018

'The Storyteller' quote is from: 'The Chosen' by Della M Cummings Wright. Edited and reworded as 'The Storyteller' by Tom Dunn, 1943. https://onceuponatime.outlawpoetry.com/2011/01/05/tom-dunn-the-storytellers/ accessed June 2018

ACKNOWLEDGEMENTS

I wish to extend my thanks to the following:

Peter Marshall (no relation) from Honley Civic Society for additional material, including pictures from Peter Bray and from the Harold Holdroyd slide collection and for his enthusiasm and encouragement.

David and Janet Stringer, who were here before us and who were able to provide additional information about the cottages and the later work of Holdroyds.

Norma Turner, a long-standing friend and 'proper' genealogist who shared the quote from The Storyteller and pointed me towards the 1939 Register.

Julian Holdroyd, who I found, by chance, after I thought the project was completed. He was able to provide additional information and pictures as well as his enthusiasm, support and the reassurance that he believes that his father would have been delighted by the project!